Smyth-sewn

A Jew Examines Christianity

by Rachel Zurer

This book may perhaps be described as a scholarly whodunit. Lively and often startling insights, based on reliable scholarship sources, come to light in this fresh study of the New Testament. The author brings warmth, compassion and humor to a sensitive subject.

Christians and Jews will find this simply written and well-researched work absorbing and illuminating.

The unfortunate anti-Judaic legacy (now being utilized in Middle East politics) has been causing concern to Christians of good will everywhere. They can learn here how that legacy arose and developed. Perplexed and troubled Jews will discover, many of them for the first time, the explanation for two millennia of antisemitism.

A JEW
EXAMINES
CHRISTIANITY

by
Rachel Zurer

Jenna Press
New York, N.Y.

Jenna Press
37 W. 8th St.
New York, N.Y. 10011

Library of Congress Cataloging Data

Zurer, Rachel
  A Jew examines Christianity.
  Bibliography: p. 180
  1. Christianity — Controversial literature.
  2. Christianity and anti-semitism. I. Title.
BM590.Z87 1985   201   83-82999
ISBN 0-941752-01-1   Softcover
ISBN 0-941752-03-8   Hardcover

Dedication

To all those, Christians and Jews
whose scholarship and wisdom
helped me write this book

CONTENTS

A JEW
EXAMINES
CHRISTIANITY

I

GENESIS
INCIDENT IN GREENWICH VILLAGE

On that hot Saturday afternoon as I walked along 8th Street with the slowly moving crowd, I heard an interchange that startled me.

Nowadays 8th Street, in the very center of Greenwich Village, is a busy mart selling books and records, jewelry, shoes, clothing and fast foods.

The narrow sidewalk shimmered with movement and color as visitors from the suburbs, other states and even other countries filled it with life and sound.

Directly in front of me, a slim girl in a blue striped cotton dress turned to her companion. I saw her face in full. The pale skin, dark hair, and alert intense expression looked very familiar and not only because I recognized her as Jewish.

My attention was momentarily caught by a tangle-haired woman in a long shabby skirt. In a loud voice, she was scolding someone who lived in her mind. A huge black man turned briefly to look at her and I stared at him. He had a towering head thatched with thick ropy braids. A Rastafarian, probably.

Coming towards us as we headed west, was a stunning youth. He moved gracefully, his expression aloof, his Afro coiffure high. A tan silk shirt was open down to his waist and real gold chains gleamed on his brown satin skin. Someone's darling, I guessed.

1

The pizza and ice cream cone eaters went on eating and the soda drinkers put cans of coke or root beer to their lips.

Just ahead in front of Whalen's drug store on the corner of Sixth Avenue, a group of young people, five in all, moved about. They seemed charged with excitement as they hopped and skipped to and fro on light restless feet. Yet they always stayed close to one another. Out of towners in their late teens or early twenties they all wore the customary jeans and T-shirts. Except that their T-shirts bore the imprint: JESUS LOVES YOU.

One of them, a fair-haired girl with a pert face darted out to the young couple ahead of me. I heard the exchange as the missionary danced lightly alongside the girl. "Won't you let me tell you something about Jesus. ." she began.

The girl from Queens or Long Island or wherever, turned her head. She glanced at the imprint on the T-shirt and without halting her stride, said clearly, "Fuck Jesus."

The proselytizer retreated, open-mouthed. She ran back to the shelter of her group after a plaintive "I don't know why you should say that."

I remembered 1948 and the young girl I had interviewed then. Could this present young woman in the blue cotton stripe be her daughter? The resemblance was there... Or was she simply a daughter of the Jewish people, 1980's style?

Had I myself been thus accosted, decades earlier. I would have murmured "sorry" and retreated, suppressing my anger. But this is now. This is the close of a century in which the State of Israel came to life and six million children of Israel were put to death. It is the close of a century in which the dominant religion of the western world has lost much of its complacency and self-respect. It is a time when an outraged young woman can say what she did.

It is 1948 and I am interviewing that long ago girl. Call her Anna Berger. Her true name does not matter; we shall not meet her again. The Jewish agency which employed me cared for concentration camp survivors. Anna was one of them.

When she left the office, I recorded our interview in her case record. It contained also these few sentences which I have been unable to forget.

"The cart is full. The women's naked bodies are on top. The cart is jolting over the cobblestones. The women's breasts jiggle up and down and from side to side as if they were alive. . . I can't get it out of my mind."

That week I registered for a course in Jewish studies, my very first.

By the third session, I came across an astounding fact, a revelation. I learned that three-fourths, maybe more of the Christians' Bible was our own Hebrew Scripture. The Psalter which sounds so non-Jewish was simply a collection of our own Psalms. Ecclesiastes, surely a Gentile book was our own Koheleth, meaning Preacher or Counselor. And all those Church words like presbyter, episcopal, deacon and countless others were words taken from our Hebrew Bible and translated into Greek about the third century before the Christian era for Greek-speaking Jews who had forgotten their Hebrew. Fantastic! Hallelujah, Jubilee, and Hosanna were untranslated Aramaic or Hebrew.

When in my reading at college or elsewhere, I had come across some awesome words from Micah, Amos or Isaiah, I did know that these were Hebrew prophets. But the mighty words were always quoted in some context which made them seem to be an exclusive Christian possession. I would slink off, figuratively speaking, uneasy and uncertain, bowing to Christian poise and assurance of ownership.

But now, after Auschwitz, I was taking a course in Jewish studies. Where had I been all those years? I know where. I had been in hiding as a Jew. I had kept busy absorbing all I could of American and European literature, foreign languages, psychology, history. . . .

In 1948 then, I was a moderately well-educated American and a grossly ignorant Jew, that painful and ambiguous part of my identity. I knew the principal Jewish holidays but I did not observe or understand them in any depth. I used the phrase "Old Testament" for Hebrew Scriptures just as everyone did in my world. All my Jewish friends came from the same milieu; our immigrant parents were poor and no longer pious.

Except in books on ancient history, I do not remember any

reference to Jews. As one writer put it "They (the Christians) succeeded in sweeping the Jews out of history."

Except that the Jew was planted firmly in English literature in the unforgettable gabardines of Shylock and Fagin.

The reading list for my 1948 Jewish studies class included the Bible, of course. I borrowed one, the King James version. Was there any other? I read through parts of the "Old Testament". Then in a burst of daring, I skimmed the gospels, all four of them.

I was impatient to get to my next session. I had made another discovery.

Even now, decades later, I remember our teacher. At our first meeting he had said, "Call me Mr., not Dr. Bernkrant." He had given up the rabbinate and was teaching now at this leftish school. I did not know how far left it leaned and I did not care.

"Dr. Bernkrant," I called out boldly. He was writing on the blackboard.

"Yes?" he asked without turning around.

"Dr. Bernkrant" (I could not call him Mr.), "I just read the gospels."

"Fine," he replied indifferently and continued chalking.

"I have just discovered"—I arrested him with the urgency in my voice—"I have just discovered that the reason for antisemitism is Christianity."

At this, he turned around. He was speechless. He actually put up an arm as if to ward off a blow. Finally he muttered in a stifled voice. "I didn't say that."

"I know you didn't," I reassured him. "I did." I went on talking, oblivious of the others, of him. What I had to say, needed saying. Of that I was sure.

"Why haven't they amended the New Testament?" I asked in outrage. "Why has it gone on so long without change. It's full of hatred, hatred of Jews, especially in Matthew and John."

"I, I . ." he stammered unable to say another word. His face seemed to disintegrate, the way a completed jig-saw puzzle disintegrates when the table is jarred. He stared for a few seconds then he reassembled his features and turned back to the chalkboard. "That subject," he said shakily, "is not a suitable one for this class." He picked up a second piece of chalk, still holding the first, and unsteadily underlined the name of the first Jewish king, Saul 1030 B.C.E.

That incident took place many years ago. What did I do with my special revelation? I did nothing. I raised my children and continued to work at one job or another in my field. And what did I feel about my Christian friends and colleagues and later my Christian relatives by marriage? Did I become bitter, avoid contact, nourish anger? Not at all. It never occurred to me to connect these loving and well-loved people with Matthew and John. They apparently made no connection either.

With my new knowledge, scanty as it was, I became somewhat less self-hating. There are degrees of self-hate, ranging from shame and contempt for oneself and one's fellow-Jews all the way to suicide.

During these years and until the incident on 8th Street, I was engaged by the fascinating world around me. It was full of nonsectarian pleasures and treasures: books, theater, travel, concerts, museums and later the wonder of television.

Which of us ever defined Walter Cronkite or Phil Donahue — to name the very first examples which come to mind — by his religion? Or who can read Russell Baker in the New York Times without having one's toes curl in non-sectarian delight. These and many, many others like them of all races, religions and nations can invoke in us a simply human response to their warmth, humor and lovingkindness. The divisiveness which religious separateness brings about does not exist.

That same hot summer, I attended a week's seminar in a Cornell University Alumni program. *Literature of the Holocaust* was the title of the course. The associate professor who gave the course must have been a toddler when the events took place. He knew the literature but the class of eight Jewish men and women and three Catholic women took over. In spite of his pleas to talk literature, we insisted on turning the sessions into a series of discussions. Why did it happen? Could it happen again? (Our earnest young professor managed to introduce the prose and poetry of the Holocaust into the discussions anyway.)

One evening a fellow student, one of the three Catholics and I were sitting in a campus bar with a gin and tonic hoping to cool

off. My companion was a good-looking woman with a very fair
skin and hair of the same color brushed off her forehead.

"How you must hate us!" she said suddenly.

The straw dropped from my mouth. "Hate you?"

"Because of what happened. You know. . ."

Of course I knew. We both knew. We had read and talked of
the methodical murder of men, women and children because
they were Jews, not Christians. We had talked of the phrase,
"man's inhumanity to man" and found it a piddling gush of
words, empty of real meaning. It presumed that man had humanity. That Hebrew psalmist who marveled "what is man that you
have made him little less than divine" (8:6) had not anticipated a
Christendom which would vilify his descendants.

Innocent children born into Christian homes, having been
taught that Jews had cruelly killed their loving Savior, could stand
by indifferently. Some few might even find a vengeful gratifica-
tion. I think of that midwesterner who said he had been taught in
his church that Jews were evil. He had also been taught that evil
should be eliminated. He was unmoved by the Holocaust.

Searching for an honest answer to my fellow student's half-
query, I found that far from hating her, I had a strong feeling of
warmth for this concerned fellow human. But I recognized a
corollary of truth in her sad comment "how you must hate us". I
recognized the profound anger I felt not at Christians, but at a
Christendom which had for centuries harried hapless Jews from
one corner of their Christian domain to another, robbing, extort-
ing, exiling, torturing and killing when it was convenient to their
purposes.

Jews had been limited to occupations which had made them
further vulnerable to hatred and scorn. Yet, when left in peace,
Jews would prosper because of their level of civilization, their
standards of morality and their urge to survive. Undoubtedly
they bent their every effort to evade or circumvent their oppressors but they could not combat a powerful and punishing majority. Jews survived also because there were periods of freedom
from persecution when they could regain their breath before the
next onslaught.

As was plainly stated by the Church Fathers, continuing the

anti-Judaic precedents in the now sacred New Testament, the lot of the Jews was to suffer misery, reprobation and enslavement for denying that Jesus was Savior and that Christianity was the one and only true religion.

During those long dark centuries, there were humane Christians who took to heart the ethics of their "Old Testament". But they were still too few in number among those peoples who had been coerced or nudged into Christianity. Scholars agree that the history of Christendom vis-à-vis the Jews had been an ugly one.

After that brief seminar at Cornell, I became restless. I had time now. My nine-to-five days were over. My family responsibilities were light. My mind was teeming with memories, experiences, observations and ideas straining for expression.

"What would you like to do?" I asked myself one day. "What interests you most?"

"Being a Jew interests me most" was my immediate response. "I want to know what being a Jew means to me and to others like me."

So I began to read. I read steadily and methodically and with ever increasing interest. Early Christianity kept me enthralled as I followed its progress from being a small sect within Judaism until it was acknowledged by Rome three hundred years later. (I noted, in passing, that it had also taken three centuries from the landing on Plymouth Rock to the landing on the moon.)

Gentile Christianity, though younger than the Jewish religion by more than a thousand years, was now much more numerous, far richer and tightly organized as Judaism has never been.

During my years of absorbed and fascinated reading, I digested the contents of several hundred books, skimmed or scanned several hundred more before I began writing. And as I wrote, I continued the use of reference works, newspapers, periodicals and encyclopaedias.

Some startling conclusions resulted from my intensive study of the New Testament. These are discussed in later chapters.

A rich diet of Christian and Jewish scholarship had nourished me during these years. After this intensive study, I rejoined humankind as an authentic Jew. An authentic Jew I define as one who is genuinely comfortable about his identity in a non-Jewish environment. He does not have to be observant or orthodox in order to be authentic. He does have to know his own religion and it helps enormously to know and understand the dominant religion of his native country.

The Bible is the national literature for an Israeli. For us, the majority who live outside of Israel, it is our ancient history and our religious history. As religion, it is shared by the great number of non-jews for whom it is also a heritage.

Interestingly, my studies in early Christianity taught me more about Judaism, I feel, than a course in Judaic studies alone might have. The knowledge I obtained was truly liberating. I developed a great respect for Judaism and Jews, a respect which the Church had been at great pains to erode over the many centuries of its domination.

Jews are no longer in thrall, no longer subject to the ancient and repeated admonitions of the Church Fathers who warned that Jews must be kept in a state of "perpetual misery, reprobation and enslavement."

It was the "enlightenment" which freed not only many Christians but coincidentally the Jews along with them. But the effects of the negation of the Jews, begun in the second, third and fourth and fifth century by Church Fathers, took its most frightful toll in the twentieth century.

In order that the destructive demoralization of man which occurred under Hitler not re-occur, the Jew must remain liberated fully and authentically. He can take a positive role in his liberation by becoming an informed Jew. His self-esteem so forcibly wrested from him by the Church can be restored. He must understand why he was the innocent victim of centuries of assault.

Jews no longer have to placate, appease, ingratiate, apologize or bend over backwards to defend themselves. Vestiges remain however of what has been called a "ghetto" mentality. The authentic, that is the informed Jew, does not have this deformity. It still operates however, to bring anguish to the inauthentic Jew.

In a later chapter, there will be a discussion of this subject. Anecdotes and incidents will be cited of current situations which illustrate its continued prevalence. By the time that chapter will have been reached, the inauthentic Jew should be equipped with enough information so he can achieve a measure of liberation.

It was for the purpose of informing our mostly uninformed Jews — and interested Christians — that I spent more than four intensely absorbed years. I felt I had a responsibility to educate others as I had educated myself.

Understandably I write from a Jew's point of view. I believe however that my admiration for those scholarly, objective Christian writers who were my teachers may act as a counterpoise to my bias. The strong affection I feel for my Christian friends and relatives also serves as a balance.

I place this book in your hands with the hope that it will repay the reading.

II

YESHU, THE JEW
JESUS, THE CHRIST

The Jewish preacher, Yeshu, who became God for the majority of Christians did not attract much attention in his lifetime. Scholars estimate that his followers numbered perhaps 200 to 250 persons.

As for his significance, "Christians must reckon with the paradox," says noted Catholic scholar, Dr. Rosemary Reuther, "that what is for them the great revelatory . . . event, dominating the center of world history, is for Judaism . . . a buried footnote in a curious sidepath of Jewish religious history. . ."

This "buried footnote" namely just another crucifixion of a Jew, among many, by the Romans, became a revelatory event because of one man's interpretation. The resurrection rumor which Paul heard, perhaps in some synagogue of his native Greece, fired him first with anger and disbelief as he tells us in Galatians 1:13, and then with elation.

Most Jews if they chanced to hear of still another messiah claimant would probably dismiss it; Jewish history included any number of them. But for troubled Paul, the resurrection rumor touched off in him, an already heated flash point.

In the next chapter, we learn from his letters how Paul's change of feeling transformed Jesus for him into a supernatural

11

messiah (christos) who would later serve as the base for a new religion, Gentile Christianity.

The historian, H. J. Muller in his book *Uses of the Past* published by Oxford University Press 1952, describes how Jesus, transfigured in this new religion appears to him:

> "He became the Christ, a Greek word he was unacquainted with. He was sent abroad to strange peoples to compete with their mythical savior gods in a similar mystery of the Mass. He was made to demand rites about which he cared little and beliefs about which he knew nothing."

Jesus, living in provincial Galilee would hardly know any other tongue than his native Aramaic, a dialect of Hebrew. Certainly he never questioned his belonging to Judaism, a religion already a thousand years old at his birth. There is no indication anywhere that he ever thought of himself as the founder of a new religion. He lived within the community of Jews, paid his dues to the Temple and attended the Jewish assemblies (synagogue in Greek) where his comments were hardly such as to cause his expulsion as did Paul's later. If he spoke against some of his fellow Jews, exhorting them to follow the spirit of the Torah, he would be acting in the tradition of his forebears, the prophets. If he had any quarrels with his co-religionists, as the gospels imply, this was an in-house matter addressed directly to them.

While we do not know exactly what his preachments were (gospel accounts are unreliable and contradictory) his genuine words could only have been derived from Judaism, both traditional and perhaps apocalyptic in those turbulent days.

Scholars are frustrated that not a single word attributed to him can ever be verified. Nor has a single word by him or about him during his lifetime ever been found. Scholars believe that there must have been an oral tradition of sorts on which Mark, the first gospelist based his writing. The others copied some of Mark while John wrote a different kind of gospel altogether.

The evangelists writing from forty to a hundred years after Jesus' death probably used some oral tradition, altered and edited to agree with what they thought he might have said or what they wished he had said. For the gospels were missionary documents, each evangelist presenting his own viewpoint and bias. In this respect, Biblical scholars are generally in agreement.

Paul who was nearest to him in time, had never known Jesus. He was moreover quite uninterested in the historical Jesus; his concern was chiefly with the resurrected Christ idea.

Another of Jesus' contemporaries was the highly educated Greek scholar Philo, an aristocratic Alexandrian Jew. Apparently he had never heard of the Palestinian Jew, Jesus. Nor of Paul the Greek. They lived in different worlds although all three were deeply concerned with Judaism.

Philo, a strictly observant Jew had an altogether different view of Scripture (called the Septúagint in its Greek translation). Philo intellectualized and allegorized the concrete, literal Bible, wishing to make it conform with those principles of Greek philosophy which he had mastered. Neither Jesus nor Paul would have found his interpretations acceptable. But the early Christian writers seeking to make intellectual sense of the crucifixion story seized on Philo's work. Philo was ignored for centuries by Jews but cherished and preserved by Christians. The evangelist John used Philo's "logos" in his gospel as we shall see later.

The Jewish historian Josephus, writing at the end of the first Christian century has no mention of Jesus. Scholars suggest that he might have had some words about him but that perhaps these were deemed unsatisfactory for missionary purposes and were deleted. A later piece of writing about Jesus has been discredited almost unanimously by Christian scholars as a fraudulent interpolation.

Josephus does mention the unwarranted murder of Jacob (James), Jesus' brother, by order of an audacious Sadducee priest Ananus to the dismay of the Pharisees. Josephus gives considerable space to the death of John the Baptizer. This Jewish revivalist preacher had gained a large following with his preaching about the need for repentance because the end of the world was at hand.

The great numbers of John's adherents caused apprehension among the Roman rulers, their priest collaborators and the puppet king. It is thought that Jesus took up John's cause after his death. In that case, he would be next on their list for extermination.

Those times when the Baptizer and Jesus lived were times of unrest, rebellion and violence. Thousands upon thousands of Jews were crucified by the Romans whom they fought fanatically. Sounder heads tried to discourage the hopeless uprisings but among the rebels were those zealots who were convinced of victory. Jesus has been described as a possible zealot. And he may have been.

Dr. Sandmel, a distinguished authority on New Testament times has commented on the "ruthless provincial policies of Rome." They sent to Judea such prefects or procurators as could deal harshly with the belligerent and unmanageable Jews. Pilate is an example.

The religious aims of their rebellions were indistinguishable from political aims. The Roman authorities looked to the Jewish priesthood to keep them informed about dissidents. The Sadducees, Temple priests, had long been hated as a wealthy elite of whom the upper echelon were frequently Roman puppets. Their personal interests were best served by collaborating with the ruling power.

Gospel stories attribute the crucifixion to Jesus' conflicts with his fellow Jews. The contrary was true. Jesus was seen as a political threat by Rome. Not Jews but Roman puppet priests would also see him thus. Keeping the peace and keeping their sinecures was the aim of the priests. When the Temple fell in the year 70, the priests lost their jobs. They were not missed. Judaism continued to flourish however. The rabbis had reorganized the religion with prayer serving as a superior substitute for the sacrificial Temple rites. Outside of Jerusalem, prayer had long been an integral part of liturgy.

Rebellions continued until the final war ending in the year 135. Another messiah, Bar Cochba, had led the insurgents, supported, incomprehensibly, by the sainted rabbi Akiba. Half a million Jews died in battle; many thousands more lost their lives during this hopeless struggle. The death toll of Roman soldiers was staggering. The emperor Hadrian forbade any further access to Jerusalem which was in ruins. Thereafter Hadrian rebuilt it as a pagan city.

In Jewish communities outside of Jerusalem, the scholarly

rabbis began putting the fundamentals of Judaism in order. They purged it of the accretions of sectarian, that is apocalyptic, vision-ary, end-of-the-world writings.

The modern scholar of the Jewish Theological Seminary, Dr. Louis Ginzberg wrote of this period and I paraphrase:

> The rabbis realized that the apocalyptic view really endan-gered the moral element in Jewish religion since it lacked touch with the vital problems of man. If the Prophets had any successors, these would not be the apocalyptists who forgot the world and man, but the rabbis for whom the center of gravity was in the actual life of man on earth, not in a world beyond, important though that was. Ethics, he wrote, is pre-eminently social ethics. The vague and wild visions of apocalyptic dreamers caring only for the future world was not only anti-social but anti-ethical.

St. Augustine for whom this world was only a vale of tears and whose eyes were fixed on the city of God, provides an excellent example of a churchman whose dogma and doctrine did immea-surable damage to the common man as we shall discuss later.

Jewish apocalyptic writing reflected the visionary temper of those turbulent times. Jewish sects like the Essenes and some fol-lowers of Jesus influenced and were influenced by these writings. Scholars have suggested that it was out of this visionary ferment, out of these turbulent times that Christianity was born.

The doctors of Torah, the rabbis, scribes and other learned men returned Judaism to its orderly ways, to its concern for man purified of these accretions. "We have the Almighty and the Torah" said the rabbis. "We need nothing more."

Returning to Jesus' own time, we note the words of Geza Vermes, scholar at the Oriental Studies Institute at Oxford University. In his 1971 book, *Jesus the Jew*, he writes of Jesus' home province of Galilee: "This northern area of Palestine," he says, "a fertile and provincial land was looked down upon by the Judeans as inferior in respect to learning. It was regarded by Rome with suspicion as a land of rebellious probably zealot sym-pathizers. Here lived poor men of the soil and the sea who chafed under heavy Roman taxes and the demands made on them by the Jewish priesthood."

Vermes goes on to say,

> "Jesus' work as healer of the physically ill, as exorciser of the possessed must be seen in the context to which it belonged, namely charismatic Judaism. . . Since sickness in those times was believed to be a result of sin, Jesus in healing the sick was also forgiving their sins." He cites Mark 2:17 in which Jesus is quoted as saying "it is not the healthy people who need a doctor but the sick. I did not come to invite the virtuous but the sinners."

Vermes continues: "Miracle worker, healer and teacher, Jesus was a child of his time when religion and superstition were more closely intertwined than today." The author believes that Jesus was much admired for his powers of exorcism, for his casting out of demons (Mark 1:39) and he offers the hypothesis that Jesus was one of a number of holy men of the hasidic (saintly) type, heirs to the ancient prophetic tradition. There were other wonder-working hasids in Galilee. He thinks that the "unsophisticated ambiance" of that pastoral province was more apt to produce holy men of the hasidic type.

Like other serious writers about Jesus, Vermes has had to depend on the gospels and like other writers he selects those verses which would seem to hold true of a Jew brought up in a specific environment at a certain time in history. But there are those scholars who believe that Jesus had strong zealot sympathies. (Gospel writers seeking the favor of Rome might downplay such tendencies even if they were found in the oral tradition.) He is presented however as at one with the Baptizer in urging repentance in the belief that judgment day was close at hand. Abandonment of family and property, no care for the morrow—we find these themes repeated in sayings attributed to him. These may have been part of a genuine oral tradition.

In his early boyhood, Jesus must have known the historical fact that two thousand of his fellow Jews were crucified by the Roman general Varus in one of the periodic uprisings. He must have seen disease and poverty, oppression of the poor by the rich. And he lived during those apocalyptic times of visionary hopes and fantastic solutions.

His desire to bring relief to the oppressed — a theme always present in the Jewish consciousness — may have strengthened the idea that the wicked world would be replaced by a kingdom of God on earth at the end of days, the messianic era. Perhaps he thought of himself as the Jewish warrior-messiah. That, no doubt, is how the Romans saw him, as another inconsequential troublemaker. So he would have remained had not Paul created a "theology" around him, missionized fervently at a time in world history when a new non-pagan religion was urgently needed.

We can never know what Jesus looked like but we can use our imagination to draw a picture of someone who lived at a certain time in a certain climate, a descendant of Middle Eastern people. That he was swarthy and bearded is likely; that he had dark eyes and brows is also likely. Possibly he had the prominent hooked nose of his ancient Hittite neighbors or his Arab cousins. Sandal-shod, wearing the linen or wool garment with the four fringed corners of the pious Jew, he would have resembled most of his compatriots in a culture where intermarriage was frowned upon.

As a magnetic preacher, his personality must have been forceful, perhaps even arrogant. He must have demonstrated enough strength and assurance to convince the sick of his magical powers to heal so they could rise cured of their ailment, hysteric though it might be in origin. And to cast out demons, he surely needed a commanding presence. While all this is surmise as everything about Jesus must be, there are some grounds for this speculation.

I am reminded here of a television program I saw some time ago, originating in Poland. Whatever the political reasons for this broadcast, there appeared on the screen a number of Polish couples who were having their marriage briefly blessed by a priest.

I noticed especially one young man, a laborer perhaps, wearing a new suit of poor cut and fabric but with a flower in his lapel. He was nervously clutching one of those imagined portraits of a soulful Jesus with blue eyes and blond hair. The artful camera had caught the pathos of this young man in his new suit with the framed portrait of Jesus clutched in his rough worker's hand.

Whatever a Jew feels about Polish peasants remembering the notorious antisemitic pogroms that occurred, often after an Easter passion service, I could still feel only sympathy for the awkward bridegroom. I reminded myself that Poland was barely Christianized by the fourteenth century and that modern Polish Catholicism still lies close to the Middle Ages.

The illiterate masses that underwent immersion obedient to the command of a conquered tribal chieftain, were thenceforth declared to be Christians. They were not instructed certainly in the Jewish origins of their new religion. Their children however were instructed to learn early about the wicked Jews who had crucified Jesus their Savior. Thus when some of these semi-barbarous Christians found Jews among them, doing well, often better than they were, they meted out to them the punishment they surely deserved for being Christ-killers. They did not attribute Jewishness to Jesus. He was Jesus Christ, Savior and Son of God.

It came as a great shock therefore about the year 1905 when Julius Wellhausen, an outstanding religious scholar at the German University of Tübingen, informed the world that Jesus was not a Christian but a Jew. This news received wide circulation.

For well over a thousand years, Jesus had not been thought of as a man, much less a Jew. He was considered to be the second person of the Trinity or as God. The historical Jesus, the Jew, had been kept out of the public domain. This scholar's report on Jesus was not the first; another German scholar Hermann Reimarus had reported on this fact; the German playwright, Gotthold Ephaim Lessing, an emancipated thinker had helped publish the book in 1788 but it received little attention even from the clergy.

Now late in the twentieth century, it surely is common knowledge. Yet. . One Saturday afternoon, a few years ago, looking for shelter against a sudden storm, some friends entered a tiny church on Cape Cod. The minister was holding forth to his huddle of congregants: "Now you all know," the amiable cleric wagged his finger at them, "that Jesus came from a good Christian family."

I think also of that ghetto child, a fourth grader who had been kept after school hours because of disruptive behavior. Enraged at his Jewish teacher, the little boy shouted at her, "Jew," he screamed, "You Jew." He could think of no more deadly epithet.

His overworked and overstern teacher, responding to her own historic anger, descended to his level. "Your Jesus was a Jew."

"He was not. He was not," the boy shouted in a fury of rage and frustration.

"Ask your priest," his teacher said as he hurled himself from the room.

A sorry exchange indeed between a small boy already taught that the word "Jew" is equivalent to an insult and a grown woman embittered by a never ending lie. Both have been damaged.

That child came from what is evasively called a "culturally deprived" environment. It will take an infinite amount of educational and social resources to make him a happier child. It will take a conscience-stricken Christendom to undo the damage it has wrought in his mind.

Perhaps Jews and Christians can arrive at an interim agreement: two Gods, separate but equal, one for Jews and one for Christians.

While this suggestion appears frivolous, it is actually a de facto situation. Catholics and Fundamentalists appear to find Jesus or Christ interchangeable with God and more frequently called upon. Jews continue with their God.

In my reading, I learned that the Trinity concept had been sweated over for years and years. It seems to be ignored lately, perhaps because the Trinity has never satisfactorily added up to one. But it is a metaphysical problem and more properly the concern of theologians, not an average Christian.

Similarly, I suppose, the Incarnation problem is best left to clerics and theologians. Religious observance and church attendance serve adequately since they are a cultural bond among practitioners of a like faith.

In reading the biography of Billy Graham, the veteran evangelist, written by Marshall Fraidy, I especially noted the reply which Mrs. Graham gave to the author's inquiry: "What does Billy do when he has doubts?" She replied, "If Billy has any doubts, he simply does not entertain them." I wonder if that is true of Christians generally.

Monotheism as understood by Jews is uncomplicated and unquestioned. It remains a powerful and established concept won after centuries and centuries of struggle, won after submitting to the thundering disapproval of the Prophets who castigated Jews for occasional backsliding during those ancient days when heathen, with their women and idols, lived so temptingly close. Its simplicity, its unyielding certainty is also its strength.

I think of that six-year-old boy whose best friend, a Catholic child, had told him solemnly that Jesus was God's son. Little David waited for his grandfather to come home from Minhah, afternoon prayers, to ask him about this astounding news. His zayde (grandfather) knew everything about God. "Zayde," he said eagerly when he saw his grandfather at the door. "Mikey told me that God is Jesus' daddy. Is that true?"

To David's stunned surprise, his grandpa slapped him hard on the cheek. As the little boy stood there, mouth open and eyes filling with tears, the Zayde snatched him up, embraced and kissed him in remorse. "Oh, child, child," he grieved. Then he had his grandson repeat after him first in English, then in Hebrew, "Hear O Israel the Lord our God is one God." To this devout Jew, his beloved grandson had committed a blasphemy. He purified his lips by having him recite the Jew's confession of faith.

What are some of the data, painstakingly assembled about Jesus that are currently presumed to be correct? According to the Christian calendar, he was born 4 B.C., this small absurdity being due to the error of one Dionysus Exiguus, a monk who in the sixth century was equating church with Roman time. As for the day and month of his birth or death, these are not known. December 25 had long been celebrated as the birthday of the Roman god, Mithras. The day was taken over by church leaders and declared to be Jesus' birthday. Whether this was done to please Rome when it was decided upon in the fourth century is not known. During the week of December 17th, Romans also celebrated Saturn's day, the Saturnalia, a winter solstice festival with gift exchanging and licentious carnivals. Perhaps the church hoped to discourage Christian participation by giving the holidays a religious significance. Gift giving dates from that period. (In this country and in western Europe, Christmas did not become a common custom until the nineteenth century.)

Jesus' death occurred between the years 26 and 36, this being the period when Pontius Pilate served as procurator. The year 29 has been suggested, Jesus' age as 33. But a verse in the gospel of John suggests he was older, "not yet fifty" (John 8:57).

His mother Miryam or Mary bore other children according to Matthew (Mt. 13:55), named Jacob (James), Judah, Simon and Joseph. Several sisters are mentioned but their names are not given. The Catholic Church refers to Jesus' siblings as cousins.

As we said, there were no recorded reports about Jesus during his lifetime. The speeches attributed to him in the gospels were written by the evangelists from forty to one hundred years after the estimated date of his death.

The Roman historian Suetonius writing about the year 100 mentions disorders during the reign of Claudius (41–54) incited by followers of one Chrestus.

Tacitus, writing somewhat later refers to the "detestable super-stition of the sect," followers of one Christus who were really responsible for the great fire at Rome in 64 for which Nero was blamed. (During this pre-Pauline and pre-Gospel period, there was no clear cut distinction between traditional Jews and the sect of Jews which followed Jesus as messiah.)

These two items by later Roman historians afford some secondary evidence that Jesus existed.

Another piece of possible evidence is the insertion by rabbis at the end of the first century, of a malediction upon those sec-tarian Jews (minim) who attended services in order to proselytize for their belief that a messiah had come. This curse, placed among the other eighteen benedictions (Shemoneh Esra) recited daily, would flush out those sectarians. Although the name of Yeshu is not mentioned, scholars assume that this was the messiah for whom the *minim* were proselytizing in the synagogue.

And we have Paul writing some decades after Jesus' death who tells us in his letters that he knew Peter (presumably the same as the Aramaic Cephas) who was Jesus' disciple.

I was surprised therefore that a young woman librarian, noting the books I was borrowing asked me quite seriously whether I thought Jesus had really lived. I told her that generally, scholars believed there was enough peripheral evidence to believe he had.

As for the words attributed to Jesus in the gospels, not one can be proved to be his says the noted theologian, Dr. Rudolph Bultmann. We have to say that neither can they be disproved although most serious scholars will not venture to make positive identifications. One German scholar, Dr. Schmiedel, in 1901 was certain that only five passages in all four gospels were indisputably Jesus'. Others of course disagree.

Most however are in agreement that the gospels reflect the aims of the Church and do not give any truly reliable data about their subject. The contradictory facets of his personality and the contradictory pronouncements attributed to Jesus as presented by the four evangelists, have caused much disagreement and endless writings during the last two centuries or so of Biblical scholarship.

Leaving the scholars to their never-ending research, we look at the people for whom the name of Jesus hàs become, after almost two thousand years of pious promotion, something to pray to, to believe in, to be moved by. Adulation, adoration repeated almost to the point of idolatry, daily, weekly and sometimes hourly invocation of his name in prayer and supplication, at moments fraught with emotion, have fixed his name as nothing else could. Even if he had never existed, the effect would be the same. A few scattered films and plays in recent years have tried to fracture the image but they had little lasting impact.

The concept of a divine being to whom human things happened like birth, suffering and death, bonds the image of Jesus closely to everyday people who have the same experience. The god part of this human-god figure offers love, forgiveness of sin and mysterious power.

Among Catholics, the image of a Holy Family is a further source of connection and identification. What small child in Sunday school will fail to identify with the rounded infant held in the arms of a beautiful adoring mother while angels hover above.

Critics may derogate such groupings as characteristic of a naive society. They will recall that the image of the goddess Isis holding the infant Horus was approved for early Christian use as a portrait of Mary and the infant Jesus.

Christians who have said that they find Judaism too austere probably did not see the musical *Fiddler on the Roof*. It was based on some of Sholom Aleichem's tales about Tevye the impoverished and unlettered but devout milkman.

Tevye addresses God with intimacy, love, reproach, humor but above all with trust. Older generations of Jews especially those from the small towns of Central and Eastern Europe whose mother tongue was Yiddish (almost all of them were murdered in the Holocaust) would address God in terms of endearment. In effect, when they appealed to him as 'dear, sweet, little God,' they were saying, "Listen, God baby, I'm in trouble; I need you."

That same Jew addresses God quite differently on the awesome Day of Atonement or Yom Kippur. Then he is in the exalted presence of the Almighty. He uses not Yiddish, but Hebrew, the Holy Tongue. That troubled teenager I observed at a tent meeting in southern Georgia must have felt as close to Jesus as Tevye did to God.

About a hundred people were gathered inside the tent, half of them black. The consumptive looking preacher was white. Sitting one place from me was the teenager, a girl of about sixteen with a softly rounded face and a clear brown skin. In the row ahead sat her mother and younger sister. I could tell this was a family from the small movements and glances. The mother looked tense and forbidding; the younger sister relaxed and indifferent.

My bench companion seemed unaware of anything but her grief. She kept clasping and unclasping her hands as she murmured "Jesus, O Jesus" over and over. I longed to talk to her, offer some help or comfort but of course, I did not dare. She kept murmuring her magic word, her mantra. If her troubles were resolved, she would say fervently, "Thank you, Jesus. Oh, thank you, Jesus." If not, she would not reproach or blame the magic name.

Other incidents at that meeting were distressing. The minister looked sickly and the congregation poor. He pressed them to part with their money (which he undoubtedly needed) and they were generous.

He spoke emotionally of Jesus using the familiar stock phrases:

"Believe in Jesus and he will take all your troubles away, Jesus loves you; He will take away your sins!" In a sermon devoid of any content but uttered as semi-hysterical quaverings, he stirred up feelings. There were indeed many feelings, all close to the surface. One after another of his listeners got up, almost all women. Spasms shook some of them as they stood, arms outstretched. The preacher would hasten to one who seemed most shaken, speak burningly of Jesus, then push her backwards, pressing the heel of his hand on her forehead.

His two lady deacons holding a large cloth would help lower the enthusiast safely and then quickly cover any unseemly display of flesh or underclothing. When the spirit left the ecstatic, she would get up and return to her seat, flushed and gratified.

I was witnessing what must have happened in those early assemblies in Corinth or Antioch or Ephesus when Paul's new converts felt the spirit or babbled in tongues. This must have been as common in the mystery cults as they are even today in primitive societies. In so-called advanced civilizations, the same emotional expression of feelings occurs among some Pentecostal groups.

Whenever Jews meet, especially those of the older generation, there is a possibility that the subject of religion will come up. And so it happened at an informal dinner one day. We were six Jews; one an avowed atheist, one a scholarly observant Jew and the others, secular, humanist, agnostic or all three. We still had questions about the dilemma of a Jew in a Christian world. Our children, almost half of whom had married non-Jews, seemed to have no questions, none at least that they confided in us. They had little interest in religion at all. Or so they said.

"Do you think we ought to take back Jesus?" our psychotherapist friend Dorothy asked after clearing her throat.

We were startled although the idea was not at all a new one. But it seemed irrelevant, even incongruous.

"Whatever for?" Ellen our lawyer friend asked. "He doesn't belong to us. Certainly Jesus Christ does not."

"Why upset the Christians?" asked Arnie our atheist. He is a blunt plain-spoken man, self-educated and successful in business.

"They have spent almost two thousand years promoting him. He is the Christians' God. We don't need him; we have our own." At this remark of our atheist, we all burst into laughter. "Even if we don't believe in God." Arnie amended sheepishly.

"He never left Judaism," our scholarly Robert put in. "But I agree with Arnie. He belongs to the Christians now. Besides," he added, "he has nothing new to tell us."

"How about loving your enemy?" Lillian challenged him. "We don't have that in our Bible."

"We do better than that." Robert showed annoyance. (He doesn't like Lillian.) "We have a proverb that says if your enemy is hungry or thirsty give him food and drink. We try to turn him into a friend so we can honestly love him."

Lillian persisted. "How about turning the other cheek. We don't have that."

Ellen who is a lawyer answered. "There was an item in the New York Times a while ago about a Jewish lawyer who sent a check for a thousand dollars to a Catholic family. They had no money to pay court costs for their son's trial. He had been arrested for defacing and vandalizing a synagogue. That's turning the other cheek, wouldn't you say?"

"Only a Jew like Jesus could have thought that one up," Arnie smirked. "Huh, I wonder how many Christians turn the other cheek?"

"Have you got a Bible? Robert had been thinking hard. Our hostess found her son's old school copy and turned to "Lamentations" as he requested. "There." Robert was pleased. He read (3:30) "He giveth his cheek to him that smiteth him."

"That's not quite the same." Lillian complained. "All right, all right," she conceded as she saw Robert's face.

"You see?" Arnie was triumphant. "Everything they say comes from our Bible."

"It's their Bible too," I told him. "They adopted it almost two thousand years ago. They call it the Old Testament."

Everyone looked at Arnie as he absorbed the news. "Some nerve!" he said at last. "Some nerve, considering what they did to us!"

Our hostess got up. "Let's have coffee on the porch."

Learned Jewish scholars have remarked that the missionary
bias of the evangelists may actually have diminished the man
they sought to elevate. The reiterated statement, "Do this for
<u>my</u> sake (that is, Jesus' sake), rather than for the sake of righteous-
ness tends to devalue what Jesus might really have said.

Christians who grew up believing that the gospels present
original truths as uttered by Jesus, need to turn to the Bible (their
Old Testament) and to the rabbinic wisdom circulating in his
time. Here will be found the sources for sayings attributed to
Jesus. (Except of course for the scurrilous words and vilifications
put into his mouth by the missionary evangelists.)

Dr. Sandmel, the late distinguished scholar of the New Testament summed up his thoughts, in part, about Jesus:

> 'I own to seeing no originality in the teachings of Jesus for
> I hold that those passages about his supernatural role do
> not reflect his authentic words. As for those teachings
> which are conceivably his, they seem to be of a piece with
> Jewish teachings in that they range from the common-
> place to sporadic flashes of insight which other Jewish
> teachers have also achieved. . . I can not ascribe to the
> teachings of Jesus a striking uniqueness which in honesty I
> do not discern.
>
> "He was in part a teacher, a Jewish loyalist, a leader of
> men with a personality striking enough . . . for his
> followers to say he had been resurrected."

III

PAUL
A JEW FOR THE GENTILES

That storefront mission on the Bowery is long gone. Lamps and lighting fixtures are displayed in the window now. But on that misty November evening when we passed by, derelict drunks were going in and out. The mission served hot soup.

My friend and I hurried our steps in the dusk, avoiding the loitering men and the sleeping bodies huddled against the buildings.

Above the mission door, a neon sign flickered, surrealist red in the moist air. Just as we neared the store, a man came out. I had time to notice that he was young with an intelligent, still handsome face in spite of its dirt and scratches. His clothing was dirty and second-hand, his shoes ill-fitting. But he was steady on his feet.

He caught our interested glance. Then he looked up at the sign. In large red letters, it proclaimed: JESUS DIED FOR YOU. He stared at us for a moment, then snarled, "Who the hell asked him to die for me!" He scuffed past us muttering "fuckin' Jew bastard."

Was he embarrassed at meeting the intent gaze of two girls not much younger than himself? Did he recognize us as Jewish-looking? Whatever the thoughts that went through his troubled mind, the memory of that encounter stayed with me.

What would I say to him now, now that I am older, bolder and better informed?

"Hold on," I would say. "You've got it all wrong. Jesus didn't die for you; that idea came straight out of Paul's head. Sure Jesus was put to death; the Romans thought he was a troublemaker. Anyone who gathered a crowd was under suspicion then. Religious talk was political talk. Thousands of Jews before Jesus had been crucified; many thousands more would be nailed to poles by the Romans after him. Jesus was just another one." (Until Paul came along about ten years or so later with his special idea.)

That's what I would tell him. But that poor drunk is probably dead. Maybe he died of cirrhosis of the liver or maybe he froze in some tenement hallway.

What desperate need drove Paul to seize on that resurrection idea he heard from some credulous follower of Jesus? True the atmosphere in those uneasy times was thick with talk of judgment day, of messiahs and extraordinary happenings. Jewish writings at least since the Book of Daniel in 165 B.C.E. and into Paul's times brimmed over with visions, prophecies and apocalypses.

Alienated Jews, especially in the Greek and Alexandrian diaspora were leaning towards those gnostic beliefs that encouraged ideas of mystical union with God.

But the common man, unlearned and overtaxed, poor, oppressed and fearful of paganistic assaults on his hard-won monotheism, would look to a warrior-messiah, a practical leader who would restore religious freedom and bring to pass the kingdom of God on earth.

Such as these would be followers of Jesus. Some of the simpler ones would cling to hope even after he was put to death. Everything was possible to God! They could believe that their leader Yeshu had been seen alive, in Emmaus or Galilee after his death.

The upper classes, the Sadducees and the priesthood did not need to believe; they were comfortable with things as they were.

Paul, we remember, was neither rich nor especially well-educated. His tongue was "koine," the vernacular Greek. He had no classic learning. And as a Pharisee, the idea of a final resurrection on judgment day was not unacceptable. Besides his personal need was very great.

Before we talk about those ideas of Paul which changed a small Jewish sect with a belief in Jesus as a resurrected messiah into an anti-Judaic separate religion, we should say something about this apostle to the Gentiles.

He was born about the year 10 and died about the year 65; exact dates are unknown. But unlike Jesus about whom nothing is verifiable, we do have some information about Paul from his own pen.

Of the thirteen letters extant, and making up almost half the New Testament, most Bible scholars are reasonably certain that seven are actually his. Two are definitely not and four are still being debated. He dictated these letters to a traveling companion on his missionary journeys to provide answers to questions presumably asked of him by the little assemblies he had started or was serving.

The "theology" in his epistles provided the base for later Christian thinking and dogma. The letters also give us some facts about himself. Most important, the feeling-tone of his communications provides a rich source for interesting speculation about his personality; he was a man of strong feelings.

We learn from his own words that he was a plain-looking, unimpressive man with little skill in oratory. He tells us about the "thorn in his flesh," some chronic ailment which tormented him. We know nothing about the nature of this illness, except for a statement in Galatians 4:14 where he expressed gratitude that the congregation "resisted any temptation to show scorn or disgust at the state of my poor body."

Writers have attempted to determine what his ailment was. It has been suggested also that he had epilepsy and weak eyes. It is not unlikely that he had some psychosomatic problem of the skin like eczema or psoriasis or dermatitis. Whatever troubled him, it did not interfere with his travels as a missionary.

For an outsider's description, we have a second century chronicle entitled *The Acts of Paul and Thecla*. Since the writer of this naive account clearly venerates Paul, the unflattering description may possibly be correct.

> "At length we saw a man approaching, namely Paul. Of low stature, bald with crooked thighs, his eyebrows met over kindly, hollowed out eyes and a large crooked nose. Sometimes he looked like a man, sometimes like an angel. . ."

For Paul to become the anxiety-ridden, emotionally troubled man his letters plainly reveal he was, we can not be far wrong when we guess that he must have had a painful childhood.

Plain, bandy-legged, undersized and sickly, we picture him spending all his time memorizing Scripture or working at a trade. Like every Jewish boy, especially of a poor artisan family, he had to learn a trade. There were enough Biblical warrants for this. Genesis 3:19 warns: "By the sweat of your brow, shall you get bread to eat. ." There were others.

(Centuries later when Protestants concentrated on the Old Testament, they adopted this precept, calling it understandably the Protestant or Puritan work ethic.)

Paul seems to have committed all of the Septuagint to memory. The Septuagint is Hebrew Scripture translated into Greek about the year 250 B.C.E. for the many diaspora Jews who had forgotten their Hebrew. Paul's skill in memorization was such that he seemed able to cite Scripture effortlessly. One earnest researcher found no fewer than 87 quotations in just four of Paul's epistles.

In more recent history, a Jewish child was given honey cake or iced cookies shaped as Hebrew characters so he could associate religious learning with sweetness. Paul, I venture to say, received no such enticement. From a study of his letters, I am led to believe that this unprepossessing child was not offered any indulgence. His writings which so stress the importance of love suggest his own deep and unfulfilled need.

His emphasis on sin and its consequence, death, as he unhappily believed, tells us also that he carried a heavy burden of fear and guilt. Perhaps he failed to please an overstern and rigid father by some neglect of observance. Perhaps, living in a Hellenistic environment, he may have succumbed to some forbidden sexual action.

He would surely feel both fear and rebellious anger at binding strictures. These would have to be suppressed and guilt would be his daily haircloth.

He was unmarried, whether a bachelor or a widower is not known. This would be an unusual situation for a Jew. Normally a Jew married young; if a widower he would remarry. Also unusual for a Jew was his abnormal association of sex with sin. To Paul they were painfully synonymous and connected with religion.

The average Jew would be occupied with earning a living, raising a family and observing the commandments. Paul, however always seemed to be seeking a religious explanation for his inner turmoil. His sickly attitude about the flesh, later shared with so many Christian ascetics was a deviation from the habitual Jewish view of sex as a normal wholesome part of life. There were however some, more often perhaps among Hellenistic Jews who had turned to the gnostic-like, mystical "spiritual" movements that had arisen during what is called the "intertestamental" times, from the second century B.C.E. on.

Such a monastic sect as the Essenes which disdained the Temple and "establishment" or traditional Judaism functioned outside the mainstream of normative Judaism. This communal order, excessively zealous in its piety, was known for the practice of frequent lustration or ritual cleansing. Members wore white garments. They lived an austere and often celibate life. They were strict Sabbath observers; they believed in immortality of the soul but not in resurrection.

The sect may have arisen in the second pre-Christian century. It was then that the Syrian Antiochus IV (Epiphanes) tried to Hellenize Judea and the the Maccabees rose in revolt. After three years of intensive guerilla fighting, the Syrian armies were defeated and Judea became an independent state once more. It lasted for about seventy years until it fell to Rome. (Hanukah, the Feast of Lights or Dedication is celebrated to this day to commemorate the triumph of religious freedom.)

Philo Judaeus, a contemporary of Paul and scion of an aristocratic and wealthy family of Alexandria was one of the many

upper class diaspora Jews who succumbed to Greek culture. A
highly cultivated Greek scholar, he reconciled the Hebrew Scriptures with his Greek thinking by allegorizing and "spiritualizing"
them. For example, Sarah signified virtue; circumcision meant
the pruning of passions, the story of the Exodus was not only the
escape from Egypt but also escape from the body to a higher
spiritual state.

Influenced by Plato, he identified God as True Being, never
attainable but accessible through the "Logos," God's mind or
wisdom. The evangelist John and the Christian church used
Philo. The church preserved his works, whereas rabbinic Judaism
ignored him for many centuries.

To Philo, God could be experienced through the mind only
when it was freed from bodily senses and passions. It was this
"higher" or "spiritual" mind that could apprehend God's mind.
"For Philo the observance of the laws of Judaism was the soul's
path to God."

Quoting Dr. Sandmel further, "to Philo, the soul was a
divine part of man incarcerated in the body, and con-
stantly seeking release from it. The body, being material,
bound one to the material world, and being mortal, obli-
gated one to die. In its fullest sense, "salvation" meant the
escape from the world and from death."

But, Dr. Sandmel points out, Palestinian Judaism
never conceived of man as requiring such "salvation." This
need for salvation is based on the premise that the material world is evil. Judaism insists it is good and mankind has
no need for salvation. "But for Philo and Paul, influenced
by their Greek world toward the idea of transcending
physical nature, salvation from the material world was the
focus of religious aspiration."

For Paul, Jesus served as that "Logos," that aspect of
deity which could be apprehended by man. God had graciously provided man with salvation, said Paul, if he would
believe and identify with Jesus Christ.

Unlike Philo, Paul was not an intellectual. He was a
stormy, passionate man who longed for closeness and

intimacy with his heavenly Father, something he probably did not get from his earthly one. Though he was not a calm, reasoning thinker, Paul was keen-witted and quick. His mental processes as revealed in his letters show an ingenious though unorganized mind. He seemed to be ruled by intense feelings.

He wanted to feel free of sin. Above all, he wanted to be forgiven. The path to forgiveness and reconciliation with the Father, as Paul surely knew, requires only repentance, as Jesus and John the Baptizer insisted, and as every tenet in Judaism proclaims. But Paul could not make this ancient and reliable prescription for God's grace work for him. We do not know why but we can speculate.

Paul wanted forgiveness for his sins (real or imagined) without having to work for it. He wanted forgiveness with no strings attached, no obligation on his part. He needed to be loved even if he were "bad," that is, sinful.

Unconditional love was what he sought. This is a familiar dynamic among rejected children as studies have shown. Paul wanted to be so loved that he did not have to pay by repenting. He wanted to be given forgiveness as proof of that total love.

I am reminded here of that popular novel and movie of some years ago. In this *Love Story,* the hero says to the heroine—or maybe it was the other way round—"Love means not having to say you're sorry."

Admittedly this analogy, on the face of it, sounds absurdly simplified since it presents Paul's problem in a very elementary way. Especially because Paul's problem (along with many other sociological factors) led to a world religion. Yet I think it applies.

Paul believed he had committed some carnal sin for which he could not forgive himself and for which his capacity for repentance seemed inadequate or lacking. This sin (coveting, lusting and perhaps fornicating) appears to have affected his whole existence. He longed to live in the realm of the spirit, in a non-material, non-carnal world.

He sought to project responsibility for his sin on the Law. The Law was to blame; it aroused ideas of coveting and lusting. Then he backed off, as in Romans 7:14ff, when he said the law was spiritual but he was not. Here we find his idea, so alien to Judaism, that man is naturally sinful, that the material body is separate from the spirit and that they are at war. Unlike Philo who finds in the observance of the law, his path to salvation, wretched Paul is a slave to guilt (imposed on him in childhood perhaps).

"Miserable creature that I am," he says (Romans 7:24) "who will rescue me from this sinful body doomed to death?"

Then he tells us how he found his answer. The circumstances of the fairly recent death (within a decade or so) of the preacher Jesus, crucified as a potential or perhaps actual agitator was not in itself an especially noteworthy event in those days. We have already commented on the death of that other Jewish revivalist preacher Jokhanan (John) the Baptizer some time before Jesus.

The story Paul heard from some believer of a bodily resurrection, sparked an unusually strong reaction in him, apparently at some crucial time of crisis in his life. He was shaken. Still, as we have said, the idea of resurrection at the end of time was not unfamiliar to him as a Pharisee.

At first, he strongly rejected the idea. As he says in Galatians 1:13 "you know how savagely I persecuted the church of God and tried to destroy it": Apparently he fought a strong temptation to yield to the idea. But then as we might expect from an overwrought and needy man, he embraced it with passionate fervor. It might mean his own "salvation."

His schema had to be right, for as he says in first Corinthians 15:13–14

> "If there be no resurrection, then Christ was not raised and if Christ was not raised, then is our gospel null and void and so is your faith. ."

Paul conceived the idea that a sinless (because resurrected) being had sacrificed himself out of love for him. Paul would then be free of sin himself and have access to the Father, an exhilarating idea.

The story of the resurrection had to be true. Paul was predicating his own salvation on that death and resurrection theme so familiar to a Greek mind. As a Jew, he would see the hand of God in the resurrection. As a Greek, he would see rebirth and purification for himself.

What did Paul need most? Paul needed love most. With the familiar death and resurrection theme in his mind, Paul would develop it to have a special personal relevance.

Someone who loved him beyond life, someone who would sacrifice himself out of love for Paul and by an atoning death free the sin-laden Paul so he could have access to the real object of his search, God, the Father.

The recently crucified Jesus served as the perfect peg on which Paul could hang his construct. Call it inspiration, even revelation. It does not matter.

Jesus' crucifixion has been described by modern Christian scholars as "an unimportant and insignificant event" of the time. But for Paul, it was a watershed event. He would achieve forgiveness, his sins excused, his soul purified. He would become "spiritual" by being "in Christ." He would achieve atonement — and by extension, so would all mankind.

Paul was not at all interested in the historical Jesus. The part of history in which Jesus had appeared was of small consequence to him. What counted now was Paul's own devised world of Christ Jesus (2 Cor. 5:17-19). That new world was now operative for him. God, working through Christ was no longer holding men's misdeeds (here, read Paul's misdeeds) against them.

Now to convince others. Here we find Paul, the tireless, fanatic missionary.

In Eric Hoffer's book *The True Believer* he describes one like Paul.

"The missionary zeal seems rather an expression of some deep misgiving, some pressing feeling of insufficiency at the center . . . more a passionate search for something which is not yet found, than a desire to bestow on the world something we already have. It is a search for a final irrefutable demonstration that our truth is indeed the one and only truth. The proselytizing fanatic strengthens his own faith by convincing others."

(Perhaps we have here a clue as to why the Church insists on missions to the Jews. Are they still seeking affirmation of their own truth?)

Paul has been described by some scholars as a mystic but they do not seem to press the point too hard. He bears little resemblance to those self-absorbed visionaries. Paul was always on the go, hardworking, unsparing of himself, often irascible, harried and without peace. He defies our image of a rapt, other-worldly being, removed from mundane matters.

From his letters, there emerges the portrait of an excitable man totally dedicated to convincing his hearers of his truth. He is a passionate, fanatic missionary who uses the full force of his clever if erratic mind to persuade. Unorganized, unsystematic in his thinking, he yet compels belief by his own passion, directed by a darting but subtle mind.

As for that speech in second Corinthians 12:1-5, in which he "knows of a man who was caught up in Paradise as far as third heaven . . . and heard words so secret no man may reveal them. . ." I find it hard to believe his never to be revealed words. I suspect that he had to convince his hearers of his special credentials. His occasional statements: "Did I not see the risen Christ?" or "God chose to reveal his son to me." These seem purposive, certainly not mystic.

Always unsure of himself personally, Paul used whatever came to his mind that might impress his humble flock. Who could prove him wrong? In his zeal to convert, Paul, I believe was not above a bit of chicanery.

Paul's personal emotional needs were such that he moved in the direction of paganism which accepts the idea of human sacrifice. Initiating the idea that Jesus' death was a human sacrifice, graciously permitted by God so he could atone for man's sins, Paul regressed from his Judaic training. Surely he knew Deuteronomy 24:16 which tells us that a person may be put to death only for his own crime. This dictum appears several times in Scripture. Paul might argue that Jesus' death was a divine act, a very special dispensation. An opponent would tell him that on the contrary the Akedah, the binding of Isaac was intended as a lesson by God to show his disapproval of human sacrifice as well as a test of man's obedience to the will of God.

This pagan aspect of Christianity would appear to be its weakest ingredient. Even though highly intelligent and high-minded Christians have worked hard to elevate its significance even though there has been erudite talk of grace and Christian love, the idea of human sacrifice as exemplified by the cross remains unacceptable to an unindoctrinated or to an inquisitive mind of any religion. It appears to be a regression to more primitive thinking.

One writer talks of an ideological sentimentality as Christianity's primary weakness when compared with the sublime moral wrath of the Prophets. One Jewish scholar, the late Leo Baeck, called Christianity a romantic, essentially passive religion.

Earlier, I mentioned Paul's need to be loved without effort on his part. Perhaps this suggests the passivity referred to. One Protestant theologian, James Smart, urged that a return to the rude vigor of the Prophets would be bracing for Christianity. I do not recall all of his words but I sense that he was uneasy about the self-absorbed spirituality into which it might sink. One thinks here of Paul's helplessness in his search for God's gracious redemption.

Paul's originality seemed to consist in his combining elements of the mythic cults with the austere, ethical monotheism of Judaism.

The period when he lived was abuzz with rumors, as in Jesus' and the Baptizer's time, rumors of the end of the world. For his proselytes, the need to belong to some community where they could find fellowship and certainty such as was afforded by the sacred writings of the Jews, was a great attraction.

Paul finding few receptive ears among the Jews for his version of Judaism turned to the Gentiles as we know. Here he had some success. We must remember that Paul was preaching what his hearers assumed was Judaism. Paul thought so too. He presented himself as an erudite Jew, dazzling his hearers with his flashing series of citations from sacred Scripture.

It would be regarded as an honor to be accepted into that exclusive "religio licita" (an acknowledged religion by Rome) with its vast and ancient sacred Book.

Paul also was presenting to the Gentiles, not a mythic demigod, nor a folk hero but a real person who, said Paul, was a divine emanation from God.

Having granted Paul his originality, we must examine the essentially frail man he was. No matter that he had almost super-human endurance in his ability to suffer hardships on his many travels, that he was imprisoned and flogged, that he made no demands for himself and his companions, nevertheless, viewing him with dispassionate but not unfriendly eyes, he yet comes through as one who lacked genuine grandeur of spirit.

Passion, persuasiveness, persistence, even eloquence, yes, he had all these in addition to cleverness, but he seemed to lack that quality of altruism which seeks the welfare of others before his own. He had been deprived of love and he needed it for himself first. That often quoted chapter on love (1 Cor. 13:1–13) makes poetic reading—even in a modern rendering—its intention, to urge harmony among the bickering brethren does not detract from its effectiveness as poetry. Some unfriendly scholars have suggested that Paul is quoting some unacknowledged poet. However it is derived, it makes a splended legacy. Faith, hope and lovingkindness are words to inspire. Maybe Paul is rhapsodizing about the kind of love he would have wished for himself.

Undoubtedly he inspired many others with his idea. His influence was enormous especially after his words became holy writ, canonized. I believe however that scholars, centuries later, invested his words with greater profundity than they possessed. Thinkers may have found meanings which they themselves put there, out of their own need and their own depth of religious feeling.

We can not blame Paul for this. As he lay dying in Rome or elsewhere—no one knows where, when or how he died—he surely did not expect that the handful of letters he had dispatched in haste to the little assemblies, would long survive his death. Perhaps he had even begun to despair of his own theory that he was redeemed from sin by a gift of grace, sent to him by God in the form of a resurrected Jesus, his God-power.

There is little in his letters to suggest that he found the seren-ity for which he hoped as one reborn in Christ. He did enjoy the affection and veneration of some members of his flock as he tells us and he had paternal feelings for them in some cases. Only in *Philemon* do we sense some warmth and relaxation, when he commends an ex-slave Onesimus to the care of Philemon.

Not Paul's Christ but the human Jesus of the Synoptics, after centuries of adulation and worship became the more popular God.

I digress here to tell you about Roland Williams, a middle-aged black man who did some electric repairs for me. A competent fast worker, we fell into friendly conversation when he was done.

He told me he was a "reborn" Christian and much happier. After a domestic crisis, he prayed for help and felt an uplifting strength come upon him. He had sinned seriously and was in danger of losing his wife and children.

An early pious upbringing had helped him turn to Jesus. He joined a congregation of people like himself and had turned to missionizing during his free time. He had not regressed.

(There exist also fellowships—haburas—for those Jews who seek understanding and help.)

When we parted, warm if momentary friends, we shook hands. Then he spontaneously kissed my cheek and I his.

I have thought since then whether I would have felt as close to him were he not a black man. Did I feel this warmth because we both shared a common experience of prejudice and hate?

I am not sure what this incident illustrates. Perhaps I was thinking of the common humanity which unites us all and of established religion which divides us.

We know from Paul that he had tried but failed in his effort to be as "spiritual" as he longed to be. He concluded then that not only he but all were innately sinful. Influenced by Greek thought, he saw his material self as the unworthy part of his identity; it was the part that had base and fleshly thoughts. He concluded therefore that all mankind must be innately sinful; that this was hereditary and derived from Adam, the first who disobeyed God, the Father.

Here one must speculate that Paul may have related sin to disobedience to his own earthly father. We can only guess.

Scholars of Scripture say there is nothing at all in Genesis to to support Paul's idea of inherited sin as a result of Adam's first disobedience. That Adam's sin brought him death is absurd says theologian Rudolph Bultmann:

> "Human beings are subject to death even before they have committed any sin. And to attribute human mortality to the fall of Adam is sheer nonsense; . . . the idea of inherited sin is sub-ethical, irrational and absurd." Note also Ezekiel 18:2ff in which the prophet speaking for God says . . . "the person who sins, only he shall die."

Early scholars including the notable Dr. George Foot Moore and Dr. Travers Herford have both commented on Paul's flawed knowledge of Judaism.

When the disobedient couple ate the fruit—no one knows what kind—plucking it from the Tree of Knowledge of Good and Evil, God ejected them from Eden lest they eat also of the Tree of Life. (Apparently God wasn't having any immortals around besides himself.)

Paul's wretched idea of innate sin does not come from Judaism. Judaism acknowledges that man has an evil inclination (yetzer hara) and a good inclination (yetzer ha tov). He has been shown the Way and the Teaching whereby he may choose the good. If he deviates or sins—one Hebrew word means both—he has only to repent or return—again one Hebrew word means both—and he will be restored to God's love and grace.

The historian H. J. Muller in his *Uses of the Past* comments on the concept of innate sin as follows:

> "Throughout Christian history, the conviction that man's birthright is sin, has encouraged an unrealistic acceptance of remediable social evils or even a callousness about human suffering. It helps to explain the easy acceptance of slavery and serfdom and a record of religious atrocity unmatched by any other high religion."

Unfortunately for Christendom, the 4th–5th century Church Father, St. Augustine, another emotionally troubled man whose mother's overstrong attachment to him marred his life, embraced

Paul's idea of innate sin, elaborated and expounded it until it became the firm, fixed and destructive doctrine of original sin.

With the spread of Christianity, this inhumane thesis brought immense power to his beloved Mother Church. It was disseminated for a thousand years among the uncivilized and semi-barbarous converts during those long dark ages when the Church fought with or against dukes and princes for temporal supremacy.

The insistence that outside of the Church, there was no salvation, that the Church had total control of man's fate—life eternal or eternal damnation in hell—brought to the church establishment, incomparable power plus a vast accumulation of wealth in landholdings and revenues. An excommunication threat was its ultimate tyranny to which even kings bowed in terror.

Returning to Paul, we look at a portrait of a sensitive, depressed man, apparently lacking in humor and suffering from low self-esteem. As is common, he compensates by feelings of being special and set apart. At one point, he compares himself by inference with the towering figure of Moses of whom it was written (Deuteronomy 34:10) "Never again did there arise in Israel a prophet like Moses whom the Lord singled out, face to face. . ."

Paul saw himself as the minister of the new law of Christ which to him superseded that of Moses. Perhaps to moderate this comparison, Paul retreats somewhat by saying that not Moses but secondary angels brought the law to the people at Mt. Sinai.

This is of course an invention of Paul's for nowhere in the vast rabbinic and Biblical literature can such a suggestion be found. Paul, flawed as was his knowledge of Judaism, would know better than that.

His letters to his assemblies are sometimes arrogant and abrasive as the occasion requires. Other times, he cajoles and humbles himself. Driven by his overriding compulsion to convince his hearers, we sense that he is desperate to convince himself. He says in Roman 1:13-14, "I want to be among you to receive encouragement myself through the influence of your faith on me as of mine on you."

Paul was his own first proselyte and Paul was primarily preaching Paul.

Any opposition, any question about his qualification to teach as apostle to the Gentiles, drove him to a frenzy of fear and rage. When some members of the Galatian assembly consider adopting the Jewish-Christian proselytizers' urgings to accept circumcision, he writes hysterically, "You stupid Galatians, you must have been bewitched!" He tells them that they are living in Christ now, not under the law. "If righteousness comes by the law," he writes angrily, "then Christ died for nothing" (Galatians 2:21).

Raging against the Galatians' interest in being circumcised, he flails out against them and loses control. He begs, curses, bares his own suffering and presents his own credentials as one who received his revelation not from men but from Jesus Christ. He says (Gal. 5:12) that the agitators for circumcision ought to go all the way and castrate themselves. In Philippians (3:2) he repeats his imprecations against the Jewish-Christians by calling them dogs (buggers). Paul's outbursts must be a continuing embarrassment to the Church. But he surely never expected that his hasty letters to the small assemblies would become canonized, sacrosanct holy writ. Nor that he would become, along with Peter, Christendom's chief saint and the subject of never ending and inconclusive theologic debate.

Paul continues to argue against the Jewish-Christians of the Jerusalem church who he feels are trying to undercut him. As a Jew, not a Gentile, says Paul, he is as well qualified to preach. Note he does not say he is better qualified since he was not one of the original disciples and had never seen Jesus (except as he says, in a vision).

If his flock yielded to the Jewish-Christian urgings, Paul would be in despair. Nothing could be more disastrous to him personally than to lose his flock to them. In Paul's time, they were an active proselytizing group with Peter and James (Jesus' brother) as chief exponents of a Judaism which included a belief that Jesus was a messiah who would return.

Paul, as we know, had other ideas. If his assembly in Galatia and elsewhere followed Peter and James, Paul's whole construct would crack and crumble. Their disaffection would wreak havoc with the meaning he had placed on the purpose of the resurrection. Where would he be then? What would serve as his bridge to the Father? How would he be acquitted (justified) without that schema of Christ crucified and sins expiated? How dared those Jewish-Christian "dogs" undermine him? If they succeeded, would Paul have to revert to being an "unredeemed slave to sin" under the law again?

Here we might note that the word Torah, meaning "Way" or "Teaching" was incorrectly translated into the Greek Scripture as "nomos" or law. While Torah does contain commandments, its real meaning is "Way."

To the unfortunate Paul, the "law" was too heavy a burden. It was a curse as it was not to any other Jew.

One has only to read the first Psalm to learn the Jew's "delight in the law of the Lord." "Oh, how I love thy law!," he says in Psalm 119:97. A few verses later (105) he declares: "It is a lamp to my feet, a light to my path."

Paul complains that the law of Moses condemns to death but belief in Christ gives life. Because Paul is so deeply concerned with his personal "salvation," he seems unmoved by the deep spirituality of the prophets who urge that man concern himself with others.

Paul's repeated complaints that the "letter killeth but the spirit giveth life" tells us that for Paul, spirit is detachment from the body, from the material world, indeed from mankind. Spirit to Paul meant union with the ineffable, the unknowable. But for Jews to whom dualism was abhorrent, the letter and the spirit are one. The rabbinic or Judaic meaning of spirit or Shekhinah (a literary term for the Divine Presence) would imply communion through the path of Torah. Paul, it seems, was more interested in being a passive recipient of grace. His vehicle was Jesus Christ. Faith in the vehicle was enough.

Paul naively expected his pagan converts to become moral Jews like himself, once they believed they were "saved." He did not realize apparently that they would require training in Jewish ethics before they could become the "Christians" he wanted them to become.

Paul appears to be attached to his Jewish heritage, still hoping that "the men of my own race" (Romans 11:14) will eventually come around to his own view. Nevertheless we see that his religion is not Judaism. We read his personal manifesto, epitomized in his statement in Galatians 2:20-1: "My present bodily life is lived by faith in the son of God who loved me and sacrificed himself for me."

Here we see clearly that the Christology concept which Paul initiated, arose out of his own ego-centered problem: "the son of God who loved *me* and sacrificed himself for *me*" (italics mine). Thrashing about as he did for a solution to his sickly fear of death through sin, Paul constructed this schema. Then he spent his life working to convince others of its truth for them too.

As one who comes to Paul's letters without previous knowledge or disposition (unlike an approach to Matthew and John whose anti-Judaic words I already knew) I found myself incredulous. Could one man's emotional sickness have created this fantasy of innate sin, expiation of guilt by human sacrifice, and a resurrection myth?

On reasoned reflection, I realize that Paul's personal need and his subsequent Christology construct could never have created a religion by itself. There were many other factors which led to the creation of Christianity, some more important in actuality.

There were the little ecclesiae, many of them of Paul's founding and there were others, all ready to be unified under a firm hand. Then there was the scattering of the Jewish proselytizing missions after the Roman wars. There was Rome itself in a condition of decadence. Above all there was a needy world waiting for a sure firm established religion like Judaism with an ancient Scripture, a high level of morality and a one sure God.

Later on, as the Church grew in numbers and wealth, it would draw to itself the literate and intellectuals, especially since these would be assigned to the profitable positions in the Church.

These literate and intellectual Gentiles would also become the Church apologists, defining and refining the meaning of crucifixion and resurrection and developing that theology which gave the Church status.

Paul who died long before this status was achieved worked zealously as a missionary. He was adept at "pious fraud," a technique which some Church Fathers openly approved if it would help make a point for belief (though they disapproved of outright lying). When the Jewish-Christians seem to make inroads among Paul's people in the matter of circumcision, he warns his flock that if they accept this rite, they will have to obey <u>all</u> the Mosaic precepts. Here he slips in the word <u>all</u> in the verse (Deuteronomy 27:26). The Hebrew Bible simply has "Cursed be he who will not uphold the terms of this Teaching." It does not mention the word "all." (But the King James version, probably following Paul does include it.) Judaism knowing that imperfect man can never achieve perfection, leaves room for error, knowing that genuine repentance will restore man to grace.

In (2 Cor. 3:13–16) Paul tells his hearers that Moses kept the veil on his face after speaking with God. Thus the splendor of his countenance after that talk on Mt. Sinai was kept hidden from the people gathered at the foot. Since the splendor of God was not apprehended by them, their minds were made insensitive to God's words. "To this day," Paul continues, "a veil lies over the minds of the hearers when the law of Moses is read."

Is this distortion (of Exodus 34:29 ff) a simple mistranslation or misunderstanding by Paul? I would guess this is "pious fraud." The verses in my Torah clearly say that the people saw Moses' radiance and that when he <u>finished</u> speaking with them, he put a veil over his face.

"<u>According to Scripture</u>," says Paul, "Christ was raised on the third day." Surely he is referring to Hosea 6:2 seven or eight hundred years before the Christian era who declared that God will raise the <u>repentant sinner</u> on the third day.

Again in Philippians 2:11, Paul plagiarizes and distorts Isaiah (45:22) when he says "At the name of Jesus, every knee will bow." Isaiah says of God, "To <u>Me</u>, every knee will bow. . ."

As for that phrase in 1 Thessalonians 2:15, here we can not call Paul to account. I am convinced it is a later interpolation by a Christian editor. Paul would hardly write of "the Jews who killed our Lord Jesus and the prophets." Writing long before Christianity had taken form as a separate religion antagonistic to Judaism, Paul was very proud, even arrogant about being a Jew, a member of the tribe of Benjamin, an authentic member of Israel of the flesh.

I can easily believe that he could call the law "dung" as in

Philippians 3:8 or that he would call the Jewish-Christians "dogs" as in Philippians 3:2. But Paul would hardly think of Jews as "Christ-killers." That idea was formulated a few decades later by Mark, the first gospelist for the new church and a Gentile.

Paul was a persuasive teacher, often eloquent in his letters. Whether his hearers understood his quasi-theologic arguments is doubtful. Those plain people from Corinth, from the poor and crowded quarters of Antioch, Galatia and Philippi could hardly be expected to understand all his tortuous explanations. Not all modern theologians can either.

But the converts must have enjoyed belonging to a fellowship of "saints" or pious ones as Paul called them. They were proud to be part of Judaism, now offered them via Paul. For this was still a sect of Judaism though more and more often repudiated by the parent.

The cluster of little assemblies (ecclesiae) met usually in some member's home or other available space. They grew in number because the time was right and the circumstances favorable. Christianity became a religion for reasons which had as much to do with the times as with Paul.

The world, says Paul Johnson in his *The History of Christianity* was looking for certainties. A religion like Judaism could be the answer. He writes:

> "The Jews with their long tradition of monotheism had much to offer a world looking for a sure single God. But their ethics were in some ways even more attractive than their theology.
>
> "The Jews were admired for their stable family life, for their attachment to chastity while avoiding the excesses of celibacy, for the impressive relationships they sustained between parents and children, for the peculiar value they attached to human life, for their abhorrence of theft and their scrupulosity in business.
>
> "But even more striking was their system of communal charity. They had always been accustomed to remit funds to Jerusalem for the upkeep of the Temple and the relief of the poor. Also in the big diaspora cities during the

Herodian period, they had developed elaborate services for the indigent, the poor sick, the widows, orphans, prisoners and incurables.

"Their arrangements were much talked about and even imitated and of course became a leading feature of the earliest Christian communities and a leading reason for the spread of Christianity in the cities. . ."

Johnson speculates that Judaism might have become a world religion in a world which longed for one if Christianity had not intervened and capitalized on many of the advantages of Judaism. There would have had to be, he says, "many agonizing changes" but perhaps diaspora Judaism might have been successful.

Judaism continued to admit Gentiles into Judaism, some highly placed converts among them. But their number generally diminished and ended altogether when repressive Christian legislation penalized proselytizing. Such prohibitive legislation was enacted as soon as the Church achieved power at the end of the fourth century. Laws curtailing the civil rights of Jews were hastily passed. Freedom of thought, never denied under the Roman aegis, was banned by the Church.

In Paul's time (more than three centuries before the church became an imperial religion) he had been missionizing to convert Gentiles to Judaism—a new and improved Judaism as he thought. He was offering them the thousand-year-old Judaism with its sacred Scripture; he was not requiring circumcision or dietary restrictions. Easiest to comprehend and accept, he was offering the familiar Graeco-Oriental concept of the mystery cults, namely the death and resurrection theme. Not a dumb ox or bull was sacrificed but a real human, an emanation of the one God, whose death was purposeful and sublime. An act of love.

Membership was made easy of access. To become true Jews, they need only have faith that what Paul told them was true. Faith in Christ was all that was needful. The true Jew is not one who is such in externals, namely circumcision. A true Jew possesses circumcision of the heart. (Here he does not bother giving Deuteronomy 10:16 or Jeremiah 4:4 credit for the phrase.)

To Gentiles, Paul's facile quotation of Scripture proclaimed him an erudite Jew. That he used his quick mind and dialectic skill to restate and restyle answers to suit conflicting assertions would not raise any questions or doubts in the minds of his uneducated hearers.

God's free grace, Paul explains, liberated him and all men when he had Jesus die an expiatory death. Jesus took man's sin upon himself. Resurrection was the proof. Believe in the resurrection and you are freed of sin. But righteousness is also required. You are not free to sin. Be like the sinless Christ. So speaks Paul the man indoctrinated with Jewish morality. He hopes and believes that faith in Christ will render his pagan converts sinless too.

We shall have some words a little later about Martin Luther who found his affinity in Paul some fifteen hundred years afterwards.

I am puzzled now to understand what theologians mean when they talk of Paul's new dispensation, his new covenant whereby man now has "freedom in Christ." I can easily understand how relieved Paul felt when he discovered that his belief in Christ Jesus rendered him sinless. He was free of the obligation to the law. Once identified with Jesus, even his lustful thoughts (his particular bête noire) actually left him. Or so we infer. But what about all the others?

What liberation did an ordinary Christian have? After the Church was established, the average Christian was bound hand and foot by the doctrine of sin and eternal damnation in hell. It is true that the Church Father, St. Augustine, worked out a system of penances among other devices which would keep the sinner from the fires of Hell. This was surely not "freedom in Christ?"

Perhaps revolutionary thinkers of later ages found support for their own theories in reading of Paul's rebelliousness. I doubt that Paul ever had conceived a social concept of liberty. Paul was self-involved. He wanted to be free of what he felt as the law's bondage without suffering extreme guilt.

With Martin Luther, the matter was somewhat different, I think. The two men did have much in common, however. Both were frightened, both sinners, as they believed; both had been submissive students of religion; both were sickly and emotionally troubled men; both had keen minds.

In Paul's writings which were by that time, sacred Scripture, Luther found his wish to rebel "authorized" by Scripture. The thesis of "justification by faith" was exactly the prescription Luther needed. He could now stop torturing his mind and body. As an obedient monk, he had taken the harsh injunctions of St. Augustine with terrified literalness. He had undertaken fasts, penances and self-punishment without relief. Each self-torture seemed to provoke a need for even more penance.

He found in Paul the idea that sin was no bar to salvation. That was just what he needed to learn. And from a sanctified source!

Luther could now defy the Devil, a very real personage to this medieval monk. He could now, as he wrote, "fart up the nostrils of the Devil" and deliberately commit infractions which formerly would have caused him to grovel in fear. But now he was justified by his faith in divine forgiveness. Faith was all.

We will recall that by Luther's time, the Church was an entrenched establishment, tainted with the corruption which seems inevitable when power becomes total.

Luther apparently had had no idea at first of separating from his Roman Catholicism. Like other Catholic reformers, he sought improvement within the Church. But the times, political, social and economic determined the course the Reformation would take. That Luther refused to recant when he was threatened with excommunication strengthened the new movement and helped the rise of Protestantism.

Paul like Luther had no plan to start a new religion. He merely offered a new view of Judaism which he considered an improvement. Like Luther, Paul was preaching at a crucial time in history.

What made both men important was that they had the audacity to rebel. They were both suffering from very painful feelings at the time so rebellion seemed perhaps the only course they could take.

They found their solution in a faith which removed from them the intolerable burden of responsibility for their sins. Jesus had taken care of that. All they had to do was believe.

Later on, cooler heads than Paul's, skilled and disciplined

church leaders and administrators filled in all the needful rules and regulations. They knew better than he that faith and feeling are not enough to keep a religious establishment going and growing. And they saw that this little nexus of ecclesiae had a very good "growth potential." It could go far.

Paul may be characterized in part as a sin-obsessed man of undisciplined intense emotion, a fanatic with a hint of megalomania whose absorbing mission was a search for his own salvation.

He became fixated on the idea that an unknowable and unreachable God had somehow cared enough for sinful Paul to send him a manifest of his love and forgiveness in the form of a sacrifice the recently crucified Jew, Jesus.

Perhaps because he believed that the world would soon end, he left behind a legacy of submission to authorities, and of acceptance of slavery. He may have thought that all would be made equal in the world to come. He also continued the prevalent acceptance of the inferiority of women, even though he seemed to appreciate their services to the assemblies.

His notion of marriage as undesirable may have been influenced by his expectation of the world's end. But one suspects that he found the sexual concomitants of marriage distasteful. He found the celibate life more conducive to religious practice.

His ideas of the monastic life and his idea of innate sin were undesirable, even destructive aspects of his influence on generations to come. Many of his ideas did great harm, until time and progress remedied the more damaging ones.

Paul died a Christian Jew before Christianity became a separate religion. His bitterest opponents, those practicing Jews who believed Jesus was a Messiah who would return faded away. James, Jesus' brother and leader of the Jerusalem group was killed by a headstrong Sadducee priest. Peter, Jesus' first disciple "departed," no one is quite sure when. His death occurred about the same time as Paul's and perhaps a little later than James'. Nothing is certain but all three are thought to have died in the early or middle part of the sixth decade.

It is possible that Peter may have returned to traditional Judaism after the death of James rather than affiliate with the Gentile Christians. The evangelists, however, made great use of

Peter when they wrote their gospels. Matthew gives him an important role as primary head of the Church after Jesus. He has Jesus bestow the "keys of the kingdom" on Peter. In the gospel of John, there is appended a chapter in which the resurrected Jesus appoints him keeper of the flock as we shall see in another chapter. In "Acts" Luke includes Peter as an integral part of the young church.

We have no way of knowing what the truth is since the gospels are missionary works written for the church's use. The strongest of the churches, Rome, claimed both Peter and Paul, asserting that both died there as martyrs. Again this is unverified and unverifiable.

By the fifth century, the Church had ordained itself as the symbol of Christ on earth within which alone, salvation could be found. Sinners, and that meant everyone, could escape the terrors of eternal damnation in hell only by strict obedience to this surrogate of Christ.

The Church used Paul's legacy of inborn sin, developed by St. Augustine into the harsh dogma of original sin, to bind and control its believers with a life and death hold. Strictly indoctrinated, hence unquestioning, church members did not think of rebelling.

Matters today in a more rational and technologically advanced world are somewhat different. Dogmas are being questioned, church affiliation has declined, the role of religion is being examined more carefully. But the Evangelical movements are increasing among those persons who, as in Paul's time, are looking for certainties in a frightening world.

God is no longer in heaven with Jesus sitting at his right hand. Instead, nuclear powered missiles, aimed at all mankind, will be stationed in space directly above us.

IV

THE CRUCIFIXION DRAMA
STILL RUNNING

We were both looking up at a nearly life-sized crucifix, the nun and I. We were strangers in a small church in Italy who had happened to stop in front of this graceful piece of statuary. Sculptured hair fell to his shoulder on which rested the tired head. "Oh, the poor man, the poor man." The pale fortyish nun sounded heartbroken as if she were mourning a lover.

I remembered a leaflet put out by a rural white church in Georgia with the title: *Meet the Greatest Lover of All Time.* A medical doctor, name and address given, described the crucifixion process in detail, from the cramps, the searing pain of torn tissue and muscle to the partial and intermittent asphyxiation. The leaflet continued:

> "This torture was indeed God's love as Jesus voluntarily sacrificed his life to bear punishment for our sins. Has anyone loved you more than this? There is nothing you can do to merit this love. Why not come to Jesus right now that you might personally know and experience the greatest lover of all time."

Admittedly this message is written by and for unsophisticated souls. The same message however, from the simplest to the most subtle model is insinuated repeatedly into all Christian minds that listen. But the guilt which the Church so effectively placed on its followers no longer exerts such influence, or is even accepted. Yet among many millions still, the message of sin and salvation is regarded as the nub of Christian belief. (Guilt often arouses anger; anger seeks an outlet. What better target than the Jew.)

A pair of Jehovah's Witnesses called on me one summer day in my upstate home. We talked amiably enough—they seemed especially interested that I was a Jew—and they offered their religious arguments with animation.

I explained courteously that I did not read the Bible in the same way they did. I offered them some iced tea but they preferred to talk. When the subject of sin arose, I said jocularly that I did not feel I was a sinner.

The woman of the pair tightened her lips. "It is written," she said, "that the person who says he is not a sinner, is a liar."

I nodded my head non-committally. I saw that this young woman had placed herself in a straitjacket. She had needs and problems to which I could not respond, not here on my sunny green lawn.

The subject of sin and guilt, so profoundly important and so encompassing can not be dealt with here even if I had the competence. But its effects on Paul and on Christians and its fall-out consequences for Jews especially, were dire.

Struggling frantically to gain forgiveness for his unchaste thoughts, Paul seized on the crucifixion story. Perhaps it symbolized a severe enough punishment to expiate for the enormity of his sin while the resurrection belief gave him hope he could be forgiven.

While many modern scholars agree that the actual crucifixion around which the whole of Christian theology is built was regarded at the time as "an insignificant and unimportant event in Jewish and Roman history of the first century" (F. S. Bratton), the evangelists, writing four decades to a hundred years later, exploited the event for its maximum use to the growing church.

The church needed to (1) curry favor with Romans (2) disassociate themselves from the rebel Jews (3) vilify the rejecting

Jews and put them in the worst possible light (4) draw proselytes to the new sect. The crucifixion drama offered a perfect vehicle. That it was a contrived piece of writing, bearing little, if any, relationship to truth did not trouble the evangelists.

Nowadays, the question "who crucified Jesus?" does not arouse very much interest. Especially not in our country nor in the English-speaking lands. To secular Christians and the better-educated clergy and their parishioners, both question and answer have lost significance.

Ask a Jew. He may bridle and reply "who cares." Ask another less irritated Jew and he will reply that Jesus was put to death by Romans who practiced crucifixion. An Israeli Jew might show a scholarly interest, little more.

Death by crucifixion was abolished in the fourth century when Christianity became an imperial religion and the cross became its signature. Until then it had been a commonplace. Slaves convicted of crimes, leaders of uprisings or potential inciters to rebellion, these among others, were subject to this punishment. Just as today in societies which practice capital punishment, the convicted person is put to death by hanging, gas, electrocution, shooting, strangling, beheading or injection of lethal chemicals, so in Roman times, crucifixion was one of the legally acceptable methods of executing a death sentence.

To an indoctrinated Christian, crucifixion may inspire thoughts of love and sacrifice.

To a Jew with none of this religious cushioning, the image of a naked man writhing in agony on a tree in obedience to the will of a "merciful" Almighty, can only be repellent. More, the idea seems sacrilegious, an affront to the Jew's concept of God.

The cross and the crucifix are common sights in the western world. Perhaps they are intended to remind the Christian of a debt he owes, like signs that read JESUS DIED FOR YOU.

You will recall the drunk we met outside the mission. Maybe he found the added burden of this indebtedness more than he could manage.

I have a sharp memory here: I am six years old and I long with all my heart to get to a playground where there are three swings.

It is a shabby place as I see it now, all concrete and litter. But it is
where I urgently want to go.

A long terrifying block separates the playground from my
tenement building. It is a terrifying block because in the middle
of it looms an enormous structure. On top of this structure, an
enormous metal cross threatens me. I risk everything and run
swiftly down that street, my heart beating unbearably with fear
as that heavy cross bends lower and lower to seize me in its
grasp.

As I grew up, I lost my fear but not my distaste.

One winter during a college recess, I visited a beautiful New
England town. It was called Salem (from the Hebrew word,
shalom, meaning peace). And it was truly peaceful-looking. A
night-long snow had laid a thick white cover on the ground and
among the deep green hemlocks and pines. The roofs of the clapboard houses were white too with immaculate snow. I reveled in
the purity.

Looking upward at the tallest and loveliest of these clapboard
structures, I saw a spire. Instead of a jovial weathervane, there
was the cross. The magic disappeared and the scene flattened
into reality.

I think of a book called *Anguish of the Jews* by a Catholic
priest, Rev. Flannery. The author explains how he happened to
write it. A young woman he knew to be friendly to Christians
noted the huge illuminated cross displayed at Christmas on top
of Grand Central station in New York City. "That cross makes
me shudder," she told the author. "It is like an evil presence."

The young priest—I assume he was young in 1964 when he
wrote the book—was deeply shocked by this reaction of the
Jewess (his word). He had been brought up to revere the cross as
a symbol of sacrificial love. That he was shocked tells us that his
religious training must have been partisan and parochial and that
the history of the Church had been cut and trimmed to omit its
real relationship to Judaism.

(The conservative Catholic church, presenting itself as the
"New Israel" long ago, undoubtedly avoided any recognition of
living Judaism. It was an antique, a "fossil" as the historian
Toynbee too had been taught.)

When I read Rev. Flannery's book, I realized that, conscientious and careful scholar that he was, his early training completely commanded his thinking. How could it be otherwise? He had been indoctrinated to believe that, though grievously erring at times, Catholicism was nevertheless the only true religion. At this point I thought with gratitude that Jewish religious thought has always recognized the many ways to the one God.

Since I began to study early Christianity, I realized how distorted the Christian understanding is of Judaism. As for the cross, I began to regard it neither with my childish fear nor with my youthful distaste. It is an object of no particular interest, except in an academic sense.

I should like to tell you about the first time I touched a cross — or rather it touched me. In 1943–44 I was working with the American Red Cross as an interviewer. Wives and parents would come to our large makeshift office to request "compassionate leave" for their soldier husbands or sons, almost always for some sorrowful occasion.

Mrs. Reardon, a much older woman than I, was a co-worker. She was an unlovely and unloving woman as I learned from hearing her dialogues with petitioners. Our desks, all in one big room, gave us little privacy.

Mrs. Reardon always wore a long chain around her neck at the end of which hung a sizable metal cross.

It is long ago and I do not remember much more about her than this one incident. We chanced to be eating lunch together in a nearby cafeteria. As we sat at a table in this stiflingly hot place — air conditioners were a rarity then — she suddenly reached for her cross and placed it on my unsuspecting forehead. "There," she cooed, "doesn't that feel nice and cool?"

Our contacts had always been brief. I was perhaps overpolite. I worked hard and I minded my business. In those days, want ads still specified: "Christians only need apply."

My response to Mrs. Reardon smiling falsely at me through glinting eyeglasses was also a smile. I like to think it was enigmatic but I doubt it.

We talked for a while about religion. She seemed inordinately interested in my being a Jew but since I knew very little, I had little to say. In turn I asked her about Catholicism, what it was based upon. Her response was immediate: "Faith and habit," she said.

"Habit, like cigarette smoking?" I asked in surprise. She was a chain smoker.

"That's right," she said. And that was all.

I know now that no religion can be so glibly summed up. I already knew about the nexus of legalisms which enmesh the observant Catholic from before birth until after death. I knew that the Church had as encompassing a system of rites and ceremonial as very orthodox Jewry — perhaps more. At the time we spoke, I accepted her short-hand definition, sensing that for her Catholicism was probably only the observance of externals, the outward signs.

Mrs. Reardon lacked the warmth, the charity and the loving-kindness which I find in my Jewish, Christian and atheist friends. I felt she disliked me because I was a Jew. Surely she had no other reason. Perhaps she feared me in a superstitious way. Was I not of my Father, the Devil as St. John has Jesus say?

If you watch late night movies on television, you may have seen a Dracula picture. Dracula is a Transylvanian demon whose name actually means "devil." In those early films, Dracula recoils when a cross is thrust at him. Was Mrs. Reardon fearful of that Devil in the Fourth gospel of John? Did she expect me to recoil when she thrust her cross at me?

No matter. She is surely dead now. But not in heaven, I think.

Charlotte Klein, a Christian scholar was overwhelmed, she reports in her book *Anti-Judaism in Christian Theology,* by the evidence of hatred and enmity for Jews even after the Holocaust and especially among German theologians. (Her book was translated from the German in 1978.) She found the theologians' pronouncements deadly repetitions of the one theme: Jews have themselves to blame for the Holocaust because they deny that Jesus is God. The deicide theme also persists.

With some notable exceptions, German theologians are surprisingly ignorant about Judaism. What they do learn is distorted by hostile interpretation, hence it is no knowledge at all. Reading their statements about God's rightful punishment, one has to conclude that their God is a Nazi.

Dr. Richard L. Rubenstein, author and professor of religious philosophy, tells us in his book *After Auschwitz* of his interview with Dean Heinrich Gruber, a high-ranking member of the German clergy. The Dean was sure that God had been instrumental in the Holocaust. What crimes the Jews had committed was not mentioned but it was tacitly understood to be the crucifixion of Jesus.

Jews having given themselves a special place in world religious history as people of the election are therefore subject to God's will. Not the Germans but God ordained the Holocaust, said the Dean. And God chose Hitler to carry out his will. This is a mysterious fact but it is a fact.

Thus rationalizes a clergyman who served in a concentration camp for his efforts to help save Jews (I seem to recall that these were baptized Jews). His admirers planted a grove of trees in Israel in his honor.

Dr. Rubenstein regarded this thinking as a "typical German incapacity to make a place for concrete facts . . . in the face of an overwhelming ideology."

Such an ideology, such deadly ideas implanted by powerful rigid adults in young impressionable minds result in a Dean Gruber. Here is a man tortured by the conflict between the inflexible partisan training he received and his humane impulses. How reconcile his humanity with the awesome ideas he was taught about "deicide" Jews.

Typical of German training was that harsh indoctrination of his time intended to elicit unquestioning obedience. We can only hope that younger generations have been allowed more freedom of thought.

An American professor of German, many pre-Holocaust years ago gave me an example of this training: A crowd of German peasants angry at some extra unjust taxation, marched on the town hall. They were armed with shovels and hoes, ready to rebel.

At the top of the steps, a minor official in uniform raised his arm. "Revolution verboten!" he called out to them sternly. The peasants turned and went back home.

We note that the "overwhelming ideology" with which the

Dean was indoctrinated did not, in his case, paralyze his feelings, only his reason.

The crucifixion drama is still running. It plays every year at Easter in churches and every decade at Oberammergau and a few other theaters. Recalling that Jesus' death has been the most publicized death in the western world, we can understand the drama's long run. In addition, many Christians actively believe that the chief protagonist is God or God's son.

If the drama were exclusively about Christianity, it would not matter; every religion has a right to its own story. Tragically, however, Christianity was born out of Judaism and some theologians still insist on keeping a stranglehold on the alienated parent.

I observe with wondering disbelief that some churches and theologians still clutch at the notion that Jesus' death was a crime, committed by Jews. Why do they insist on ignoring their gospels in which Jesus foretells his death and accepts it willingly?

Reading the gospels as an academic exercise, I would have to classify Jesus' death as a voluntary, deliberate suicide, carried out on orders from God. Even if some of the Jewish priests informed on him to the Romans, it would still be a voluntary deliberate suicide. According to the gospels he journeyed to Jerusalem, there to meet his ordained fate.

Again as a student, I ponder on why the Church nourished the deicide fable. And I realized that it was too useful a device to discard. The masses of Christians may have found the burden of such sacrificial love difficult to handle. As we said elsewhere, guilt provokes anger; anger seeks an outlet; the helpless Jews made an excellent target. This church-sanctioned hatred, this sacred hatred had for its chief aim, I think, the negation and denigration of the Jews, leaving the Church as the true, the victorious religion.

The more sophisticated and informed churches have by now jettisoned the primitive and rather simple-minded notion of "killing God." It still has some use for naive and uninformed minds. And theologians may be clinging to the anti-Judaism of the crucifixion story for practical reasons. Giving up anti-Judaism might put some of them out of the religion business.

A good friend Abe is a Holocaust survivor. So is his wife Clara. Only once did he tell me something about his camp experience, once and never again. Maybe he and Clara talk when they wake one another up out of their nightmares.

On the surface, they have made what is called "a good adjustment." They met as students in a free city night school and married. With both working, they were able to put their two children through college and graduate schools.

They seem able to live with the fact that their son married a non-Jew, a Protestant girl. Both young people were fellow students in biochemistry. Neither shows any interest in religion.

Abe had been spending his free time studying and reading books about Christianity. Perhaps his son's marriage stimulated this interest. He himself had had a good background in Hebrew and rabbinical study before the Nazis swept up and murdered all four hundred Jews in his small community in Poland.

At the death camp, Abe was kept alive because he was a brawny fourteen year old. He had the job of shoving the naked corpses into the ovens. One day, his long-handled shovel met the cyanosed bodies of his mother and younger sister. He never again spoke of it.

Occasionally he mentioned something about his wide and scattered reading. "This Chrysostom fellow," he asked, "isn't he the one who invented the deicide bullshit?"

He invented the word, I told him, but the idea had started about three hundred years before.

Malcolm Hay, a Catholic Scot historian, in his book *Europe and the Jews* writes about St. John of Antioch whose eloquence earned him the title of "Chrysostom," Greek for golden mouth.

"His homilies were used for centuries in schools and seminaries where priests were taught to preach with St. John Chrysostom as their model and where priests were taught to hate with St. John Chrysostom as their model."

"The synagogue," wrote this saint, "is worse than a brothel. It is the den of scoundrels, the lair of thieves, the temple of demons devoted to idolatrous cult, the refuge of brigands and debauchees and the cavern of devils."

"He wrote eight such sermons. For many years, Jews were victims of Chrysostom's repeated curse: God hates you."

The word he coined, deicide, product of a fourth century mind, shows how close to pagan ideas were the early Christians and how these pagan ideas still persist. The idea that a kyrios, the cultic lord, could suffer death and resurrection is apparently still an acceptable one, although weakening in strength.

When the Church became Rome's official religious establishment, late in the fourth century, the deicide idea proved useful as we have said; it provided a sanctified reason for persecuting the "unbelieving" Jews.

The great outcry raised about this "heinous crime" tells us how effective the modern Goebbels law can be. This "law" shows that the bigger the lie, the more likely it is to be believed.

Germany, where this "law" was put into practice, has had a long history of Judenfeindschaft (enmity towards Jews). Paradoxically the Jews of that country have been its most loyal patriots. This attachment was not reciprocated, obviously.

As for the crucifixion, it is not surprising that a contrived theater piece—for such it is—has lasted as long as it has. It has been the best advertised drama in the western world. Here was no simple situation of the good guys fighting the bad guys. Here the hero was no less a creature than the Christians' God. The bad guy was of course his adversary, the devil Jew. Good combating evil makes for dramatic tension, most especially when "God" is the protagonist. Even though he is killed, he is the final victor in a glorious finale of the resurrection. (I note that Dr. James Parkes, the Anglican clergyman and historian, comments that he stays away from church during holy week; his Christian conscience forbids attendance.)

Conditioned Christians are affected quite differently. Sympathy and love for the sinless, suffering, abused son of God who sacrificed himself out of love for each individual Christian is evoked. Evoked also are anger and revengeful feelings against those "wicked" Jews who mocked and finally killed their loving Christian Savior. Even though he is actually only a character in a play.

The Christian has not yet learned that his "gospel truth" is actually fiction, advertised as truth, repeated and promoted as truth, given grandeur and sublimity by means of all the arts and persuasions of music, pageantry, design, sculpture and architecture. Supported by all the emotional additives of rite and sacrament, what human spectator and participant can fail to be stirred by such a sanctified setting. A Jew would succumb as well were he not the victim in real life. For him the final curtain was the reality of the Holocaust.

It was the mutilation and murder of millions and the abortion of millions unborn. Every thinking Jew must share in the pain of devastated centuries. Every Jew must know that he has been the victim of a two-thousand-year-old lie.

Whom shall we blame? Placing blame might mitigate the sorrow. Shall we blame our loving Christian friends and relatives? Shall we blame all the warm and helpful humans with whom we have daily contact who are not Jews? Or the church writers and scholars who fight antisemitism with us? Or even the antisemites themselves, those people who love themselves so little.

I read of one Jewish sage who termed the Jews the people of compassion. It may be that our millennial sufferings have given us empathy. The term applies, I think, to all the people all over the world who feel for their fellows. Jews may be unique only in that they have endured for so long.

An incident comes to mind here. It happened many, many years ago but I see his face, my gentle brother, as he came running home from school with a bloody nose. Some kids had punched him after they called him a sheeny and Christ-killer. All that Sammy said to me in a wondering and hurt voice was "Why did Jesus have to be a Jew, for crissake." Crissake indeed.

As for the crucifixion story, it is thought that Mark gathering up some of the oral tradition for his gospel found a written piece which he used to conclude his life and death of Jesus. The other three evangelists copied the story as we know and varied it, each to suit his own focus.

The original writer, whoever he was, had a scanty knowledge of Jewish law and custom. We observe his ignorance of the Sanhedrin procedures and his timing of the event for Passover. He did plan that the Romans were to be exculpated and the Jews blamed. The false epithet, Christ-killer, would thereafter be used against Jews.

As for the trial sequence we can only assume it was included to provide a dramatic base, to suggest authoritativeness and verisimilitude for uninformed Gentiles.

From Dr. Bokser's book *Judaism and the Christian Predicament* we extract his report. According to the *Antiquities* of the Roman Jewish historian Flavius Josephus, and from the Mishna (Sanhedrin 4:1) we learn that the Sanhedrin met only in the daytime, never at night and never on a festival day. Meeting on Passover was unthinkable. The Romans even exempted Jews from appearing in Roman courts on the Sabbath or after the ninth hour or on the day before preparations for the Sabbath. Nor would a guilty verdict be rendered on the same day as a trial.

In Pilate's and Jesus' day, about four decades before the war that led to the destruction of the Temple, Rome would honor its commitment to all the religious rights of the Jews.

There is a question as to whether Pilate even allowed Jesus a trial.

The playwright was not interested in such details. And it is doubtful that he had any facts; he was interested in a drama which would show:

1) Jesus dying a sacrificial death like a paschal lamb.
2) Rome represented by Pilate as benign, reluctant to carry out orders demanded by bloodthirsty Jews intent on vengeance.
3) Jews as wicked opponents of the new little sect of Christians.

Real history tells us that Pilate was a tough hard-nosed administrator who would have little patience with a troublemaker like Jesus. His job was to collect taxes and keep agitators from rousing the people. We read (Luke 13:1) how Pilate had "mingled Galilean blood with their sacrifices."

Philo in his *Embassy to Gaius* written in the year 40, describes the then dismissed Pilate as a man "noted for his vindictiveness, his furious temper, relentlessness and inflexible self-will."

He had been discharged from his job for "bribery, insults,

outrages, wanton injuries, executions without trial (my emphasis) and ceaseless and supremely grievous cruelties."

This is the wavering milksop who yielded to the clamoring Jews.

This information about a cruel Pilate was well-known to the Church. Yet it allowed the crucifixion lie to persist century after century. It was apparently to their interest not to correct the falsehoods. The fiction was more useful to the missionary church than the truth.

In the Christian Ethiopic churches, Pilate is venerated as a saint. He has his own day, June 25.

That Jesus was put to death obscurely on some day convenient to the procurator is the likeliest reconstruction. Pilate would not have made a "big production" of it. We note that both gospelists Mark and Matthew include the warning of the priests, presumably about plans for his death, "it must not be during the festival (Passover) or we should have an uproar among the people."

Pilate probably had Jesus hustled off quietly before or after the Passover festival. Since Pilate was known for his executions without trial, Jesus was probably not given one. But if he did have some semblance of a trial, he would have had to walk through the town carrying a crosspiece. If the titulus "king of the Jews" was actually inscribed on it, we assume it may have been part of the oral tradition. He would carry the crosspiece until he got to the place of the Skull (Golgotha in Hebrew, Calvary in Latin).

Here outside the city walls — (Robert Macafee Brown, church writer calls it "the city dump heap to be precise") — the heavy upright stake would already be in place. Perhaps his mother Miryam (Mary) would be there and some other female relatives. His disciples, if they came, would be at a distance in hiding.

Perhaps when he died, Jesus did cry out with a loud voice, that first line from Psalm 22: "My God, my God, why hast thou forsaken me?" A Gentile dramatist might be more likely to use this line rather than the Jews' confession of faith, the Shema, possibly less familiar to him.

Yet Jesus in Mark 12:29, when asked which of the commandments are most important, cites as the first, this very *Shema* from Deuteronomy 6:4: "Hear, O Israel, the Lord our God, the Lord is one." Had he recited those words, uttered by martyrs meeting death, he would have been at one with his brethren, those victims who stood at the edge of the graves they had dug awaiting the bullets from Nazi machine guns and murmuring this confession of faith.

Nineteen hundred years of antisemitism would have elapsed to create this parallel.

The crucifixion dramatist to add further tension adds another artifice. Unnoticeably, he slips into the play, the falsehood that mobs on a festival day had the right to choose the convict they wished released from a crucifixion. So bold a lie so boldly insinuated in a work of "gospel truth" did not allow the reader to think or question. This fiction was inserted with such assurance that it was not noted by believers.

Scholars have searched all over the Jewish, Latin and Greek sources for any evidence that such a custom ever existed. They have found none. A ruler might grant amnesty on an occasion that suited him but never a mob. (We have also the fiction that a public execution would be carried out on an important festival like Passover.)

Perhaps the writer of the drama had in mind those gladitorial contests in the Roman circuses where a crowd might call out for a defeated gladiator to be spared instead of killed as was the custom then. Certainly, it had no application in this play. Anyway Pilate would hardly let Jewish troublemakers go free. He spilled their blood gladly.

Scholars are also questioning whether Barabbas is another invention. A dramatist might conceivably have amused himself by including this Jesus Barabbas whose name means "Jesus, son of the father."

As for Judas, a late-nineteenth-century French writer, scholar and excommunicated priest, Alfred Loisy, believes he too is a fictional character, intended to represent Jewry. Note that the words Judas and Jews are homonyms in German. When the play is presented in Oberammergau, these sound-alike words fit in perfectly with the anti-Judaism of the story.

The dramatist of the gospel play lifted the item about the thirty pieces of silver directly from some verses in Zechariah 11:12–13 written five hundred years before the Christian era.

That Jesus was put to death as a revolutionary or a potential troublemaker, just like John the Baptizer before him, seems most likely. Such an authoritative church historian as Shirley Case Jackson, writing in his 1927 book *Jesus a New Biography* makes his belief unmistakable that Jesus' death was to be a warning to future agitators. And in Mark 13, Jesus does sound like a revolutionary when he urges his hearers to be ready to "take to the hills" to keep alert and awake when the "birthpangs of a new age begin."

Whether he meant judgment day or the start of a rebellion, to Romans such words sounded exactly the same. Trouble.

He was hastily put out of the way by Pilate just as the Baptizer had been put to death by Herod Antipas some time earlier. Pilate, like Herod was not taking any chances either.

Jesus was probably more of a hothead than the gospelists writing forty to a hundred years later wished to portray him. Rome was still the ruling power.

The evangelists were determined to blur or erase his image as a rebel: They had other plans for him. He was to be the framework on which to build a divine figure, embodying Paul's supernatural ideas and incorporating also Hellenistic Judaism.

Before Paul and the evangelists interpreted him, Jesus must have been a preacher, just like the Baptizer his influential predecessor. John's following was probably larger than Jesus'. He preached the end of the world, urged repentance, recommended lustrations or immersions for a cleansing of the body (not for remission of sin) and "greatly moved his hearers" as we read in Josephus.

To the practical Romans, talk about the end of the world suggested a warrior messiah, an uprising and another rebellion to crush. "In the case of Judea," writes the scholarly Max Radin in his 1915 book *The Jews among the Greeks and Romans,* "the very existence of Rome's eastern empire would be threatened. For on the other side of the Syrian desert, there was a watchful and every ready enemy." Radin goes on to say that "smouldering disloyalty still present in the Asiatic provinces would break into open conflagration, at any sign of rebellion in nearby Judea."

We can understand better how anxious the new Christian

sect would be to palliate and placate the Roman rulers, assuring them that theirs was a non-political, non-rebellious group — not like the Jews. Paul urged obedience to authorities; the evangelists have Jesus advise rendering to Caesar what is Caesar's. The evangelists' strong hostility to the Jews in the gospels was intended for Roman eyes and ears as well as for the opposing rabbis.

Before discussing Matthew's version of the crucifixion story, we should comment on the fact that nowhere in his letters does Paul mention any trial of Jesus, nor does he mention Judas nor the pieces of silver. He does talk of the night when Jesus was arrested (not betrayed). Whether a trial ever took place, no one knows. He may have been picked up and summarily put to death. Paul, closest in time to Jesus did not know the date or details of his death. He heard only that he had been crucified and resurrected. (The King James Bible (1611) uses "betrayed" in 1 Cor. 11:23 while the New English Bible (1961) uses "arrested," the more accurate translation.)

Matthew in his zeal to derogate the Jews and appease the Romans shows no restraint in his version of the play. He enlivens his scenario with patently contrived additions. For example, he has Pilate's wife send an urgent message to her husband about a dream she had. The dream convinced her that Pilate should have nothing to do with convicting that innocent man, Jesus.

Matthew has Pilate washing his hands in innocency (Psalm 26:6) to absolve himself from responsibility. No Roman would perform such a traditionally Jewish action as hand washing. Matthew adds to the anti-Judaic propaganda by having Jesus given, instead of the analgesic, wine and myrrh, a drink of vinegar and gall instead (Psalm 69:21). I note a later revised Bible changes this.

Like Mark, Matthew has the crowd shout "Crucify him, crucify him" when they are given that fictional choice of choosing a victim. Besides the darkening of the sky and the rending of the Temple veil, Matthew adds an earthquake (as in Kings and Zechariah). But he also has the graves open and the dead walk about Jerusalem. (Matthew may have been inspired by the visionary and apocalyptic writings current at that time.)

Scholars have generally tried to discount or minimize the

malevolence in Matthew's cry of the crowd, "His blood be on us and our children!" His hatred of those who did not accept the new sect's belief in Jesus as Messiah is most fully expressed in this oath. This curse appears in Leviticus first where it is laid on those who commit incest or repudiate their parents, among other crimes; the bloodguilt is upon them. As late as the sixth century before the common era, Ezekiel also warns against disobeying the commandments on pain of death. Here his point is that only the guilty shall so be punished, not the innocent offspring.

Only in 1 Kings 2:33, and in 2 Samuel 3:29, does the blood-guilt curse descend to the offspring. Matthew had to search Scripture carefully to find this curse, dating from the eleventh century before the common era!

Let us try to view the gospels as if we lived in the first century. Let us try for a moment to erase the memory of the horrors which resulted for Jews from such unrestrained and untruthful expressions of the evangelists' rage. We must then acknowledge that the gospelists' intentions were not actually murderous. They hardly anticipated the slaughter of millions of innocent Jews. They were writing out of weakness and frustration against the entrenched handful of indifferent Jewish religious authorities who regarded this upstart sect as simply a Jewish heresy.

The evangelists wrote like the angry believers they were. Their words though spiteful and mean-spirited were not murderous in intent. How could they be? They did not dream that those words and sentences of theirs would ever become canonized, hallowed, sacred, sacrosanct; that they themselves under their pseudoynms would become sainted by a Church which had not even been recognized as legitimate by Rome.

Until the year 135 c.e., Jerusalem was still the Jews' religious and national center even though the Temple was gone and the population scanty and scattered. Jews were living all over the Roman Empire, in parts of Palestine, Asia Minor, Spain and in lands which would later become France and Germany, Italy and England. Many Jews were resident there far longer than some of the "native" inhabitants.

With time and the accession to power of the new, now legitimate Christianity about three hundred years later, anti-Judaic activity, heretofore chiefly verbal in the writings of the New Testament and the Church Fathers, began to be implemented in earnest. Legislation was enacted at once to deprive Jews of their civil rights. Freedom of thought, never repressed by Rome was an early Christian innovation. Scattered and unorganized Jews everywhere began to feel the punishing hand of the Church. With petty vengefulness, the Church, now having the upper hand described their erstwhile superiors as the "fecalis secta" among other insulting appellations.

The Church, greatly helped by Matthew's administrative skills as we note in his gospel, became an organized power as Judaism never had been. Even though it was now stronger richer and more numerous, the Church never relaxed its vigilance. Like any establishment, especially a totalitarian one, it dared not allow dissent, neither among Christians nor Jews.

Returning to our account of the crucifixion, we might consider now why the Passover period was chosen by the dramatist for his timing of the story.

Jesus would be in Jerusalem at this important Jewish festival. A paschal lamb was sacrificed at Passover. Jesus could be that lamb. Following Paul's verses (1 Cor. 5:7-8) the dramatist may have misconstrued Paul's meanings. Paul, we read there, is upset by reports of sexual immorality among his followers.

> He reprimands them. "The old leaven of corruption is working among you. Purge it out and then you will be bread of a new baking, as if it were the Passover bread. For indeed our Passover has begun . . . the sacrifice is offered, namely Christ himself. . ."

Paul, we see, makes no connection between his flock's sexual misbehavior and Jesus' death. He simply wants them to live like "new baked bread" in their new life in Christ. Had he had the slightest inkling as to when Jesus died and had such an impossible coincidence occurred, Paul would have shouted it to the world, over and over. What a fantastic confirmation that would have been of his thesis that Christ was indeed an expiatory sacrifice, a paschal lamb dying fitly on Passover! But Paul does not know the date of Jesus' death. Nor does anyone.

John of the Fourth Gospel pushes the tale to its limits. He has Jesus expire <u>before</u> the Roman soldier breaks his leg, as was sometimes done to hasten death.

We read in Exodus 12:46 an injunction about the paschal lamb which is to be offered up "neither shall ye break one bone thereof." And in Numbers 9:12, we also read of the lamb to be offered in sacrifice: "nor break any bone of it." John, we see, makes sure that Scripture is fulfilled and that Jesus is the unblemished sacrificial lamb, by having him expire <u>before</u> the Roman soldier can blemish the sacrifice by breaking <u>his leg</u>.

Before leaving this chapter, we need to remark on what has been called by Christian critics, the "exploitation of Calvary." The reference is of course to the passion play, passion deriving from the Latin meaning "suffering."

The medieval passion play grew out of the liturgy of early Easter morning.

"By the fifteenth century when it was secularized and popularized and outside of the church's surveillance, it became a deadly weapon against the Jews. The passion was represented as arranged in hell by the Jews who were then involved in a hideous crucifixion scene... By the eighteenth century, the passion play had become such a mixture of the sacred with the profane, such raw burlesque, its actors given to such intemperance and debauchery while still in costume, as to invite the criticism of liberals." So writes Conrad Moehlman, divinity school professor in his 1933 book *The Christian-Jewish Tragedy.*

The Oberammergau play survived governmental suppression only on pledge of revision and reformation. It had been undergoing censorship for two centuries. The coarse humor and brutal emotions characteristic of the seventeenth century play have been levelled down to more dignified dialogue, says Dr. Moehlman.

The comic villain Judas in red wig, testing each piece of silver by biting it, then climbing a tree, shrieking and hanging himself, this is now gone, he reports. However the Sanhedrin is overplayed and Pilate is too noble, superior, dignified and grave.

The legend of the Oberammergau play has it that the villagers vowed in the 17th century to dedicate the play to God if he would stop the bubonic plague which had killed about a hundred villagers. Apparently the play they did present over the centuries had to be kept under censorship for two hundred years because it was profane, shocking and blasphemous, hardly a fitting offering to God.

I picked up a book called *A Rabbi's Impression of the Ober-ammergau Play.* It was published in 1901 and reprinted in 1934. The author was a German-American reform rabbi. I cite his words:

> "I know of nothing that could have rooted deeper among these people (a quarter million viewers then), the existing prejudice against the Jew, and spread wider the world's hatred of him than this passion play. There were moments when listening to the play, seeing one gross misrepresentation of the Jewish people after another, I felt I had to rise and declare aloud to the thousands that crowded the auditorium that what they heard and saw . . . was unhistoric in fact, false in interpretation and cruel in inference, but as Shakespeare said, suffrance being the badge of all our tribe, I restrained my feelings and kept my peace as we Jews have been obliged to do these past eighteen hundred years, obliged to suffer injustice, misrepresentation, contumely in return for having given the civilised world many of its noble characters, most of its highest ideals, all of its most sacred literature."

Dr. Krauskopf related how first he had been moved by the spectacle of a saintly man hounded by wicked people until he recovered from the daze of illusion and realized with a shock how he had been manipulated by dramatically presented lies; how truth had been disregarded and malicious vilification of the Jews substituted to stir the viewers' emotions. As he uncovered lie after lie in the text, he was horrified and depressed with deep despair.

Now, more than eighty years later, the drama has not been changed significantly. Now modern methods of merchandising are being employed to induce more and more visitors to attend this spectacle.

It is presented in a picturesque town in Bavaria not far from where Hitler took his ease. He saw the play in 1934 and regarded it as one of the most magnificent plays he had seen. He recommended it to all.

The event has proved very profitable and travel agencies are promoting it vigorously. The town is flourishing as a result of this industry; hotels and restaurants continue to be built to accommodate the huge number of people who wish to buy tickets. Twice as many requests are received than the theater can hold, it is reported.

The Christian Century took note of the 1960 spectacle at Oberammergau with a review entitled *The Play that Carries a Plague*. The critic remarked on the "racial" (I would think religious) implications of the play as well as its artistic ineptitude.

In 1970, the same publication carried an editorial called *Bad Scene at Oberammergau* and commented on the play's antisemitism.

And in 1980, the critic gave a blow by blow description of the seven-hour-long drama which was viewed by half a million persons, German and English speaking. Some of the antisemitic violence had been removed, he said, but enough remained that changes must be made.

The American Jewish Committee, helped by some Germans sensitive to the problem, is working toward encouraging changes. Several gratuitously offensive sections could be removed, they report which make the Jews even more hateful than they are depicted in the gospels. Yet even with some of the more outrageous lines removed under pressure from Jewish and Christian organizations it was the consensus among critics that the play was "unequivocally antisemitic."

The villagers may be unaware of or indifferent to the play's effect in fostering and continuing antisemitism. Apparently the Holocaust did not trouble them and the play makes money.

But the murder of innocent millions under the flag of Germany while Hitler was their elected representative must have had a seriously hurtful effect on Germans. In the eyes of the world, they are still not dissociated from Hitler and Nazism. Formerly proud, often arrogant about their high level of civilization, they will not recover easily. Some of the younger generation who are the unwilling heirs of the national catastrophe that was Nazism, are making changes in the old regimented Germanic ideas.

They should turn at once to an examination of the Oberammergau play. This play was under government censorship for two hundred years, well into the nineteenth century. Sacrilege and obscenity were the charges.

The greatest obscenity, antisemitism, still flourishes and brings prosperity to its purveyors.

V

THE GOSPELS
DON'T SWEAR BY THEM

You may recall the news item some time ago about a Fundamentalist preacher who told his flock, "God doesn't listen to the prayers of Jews."

His statement acutely embarrassed his more sophisticated colleagues across the country. The ensuing publicity — which surely astonished him — brought the Anti-Defamation League, a Jewish agency which works to counter prejudice with education, into contact with him.

I would wager that this same minister would hasten to help a needy human, whatever his race or religion. For along with the obviously distorted view he had of Judaism, he had also been taught the substance of Jewish ethics, presented to him as Christian ethics.

By the eighteenth century, what previously had been accepted as indisputable truth in religion now came under rational scrutiny. More and more, thinkers were questioning all authority, social and political as well as religious.

Bible research begun by Protestant scholars demonstrated the shakiness of the claim to "gospel truth." The phrase now has an archaic sound. Probing into areas formerly considered taboo, scholars discovered that the New Testament, Acts and Gospels particularly, had been brought into being for a very specific purpose by the evangelists.

By the end of the second century, there were at least eighty Christian sects, each with its own leaders and its own Jesus story. Since uniformity was essential for survival, it was decided to select and edit four of the many gospels, add Paul's letters and begin a Christian Bible.

The word gospel from the Middle English godspell or goodspiel means good news or glad tidings. In Greek it is evangelion.

All four gospels were composed in Greek; no one knows who the authors were. Bible scholars are generally in agreement that the gospels of Matthew and John were not written by Jesus' disciples, nor that Mark was a secretary of Peter, nor that Luke was Paul's physician. It was the custom in those days to attribute authorship to well-known, usually dead persons. For example, the Jewish "Book of Daniel," written about 165 B.C.E. pretends it was written by an ancient worthy who lived 500 years earlier.

For convenience we shall use the gospel names.

Mark, the first of the four in time depended apparently on whatever oral tradition was available. This might include miracle tales and folk stories along with some sayings of Jesus. With time, these would be altered and embellished as they were passed along. Four decades would have passed since Jesus preached.

All the gospelists wrote about the life and death of Jesus; all wrote during the period from about 75 to 150; all were serving the needs of the church which wanted to unite the small ecclesiae into a unified orthodox whole.

The four gospels selected probably came from the principal churches of the time. Mark may have written from Rome or Alexandria, Matthew possibly in Jerusalem, Luke at Antioch or Rome, John at Ephesus.

Because the gospels were essentially missionary documents, each written from differing points of view, they contain differences, contradictions and biases. In the crucifixion story, they contain outright falsification.

The Fourth gospel, that of John, differs markedly from the other three which have basically a similar or synoptic view. John wrote an essay which is described as a metaphysical tract, although he includes some details of the "biography."

All the evangelists used Paul's "theology" as the basis of their doctrinal views of Jesus. He was the divine emanation whose human life and death provided the material for their gospels. John, however, deified him in effect if not in actual words.

Since he was put to death about four decades before Mark wrote, Jesus understandably had never heard of Christianity. It was the task of the evangelists to weave him, together with his disciples, into the framework of a structure on which Christianity could support itself and grow.

They did not expect, I think, that the new Church would become an imperial religion and that the record of their hostile and often vicious disputes with the handful of rabbis who opposed them would have the unspeakable effects it did. To paraphrase the scholar Dr. Bokser: From the talk nowadays one would think that the entire world in gospel times had nothing on its collective mind but the conflict between Jews and those people who became Christians. Nothing could be farther from the truth. The quarrels were petty and of minor significance then.

JOHN THE BAPTIZER

Mark introduces Jesus to us as a grown man who has just been baptized by Jokhanan, known to Christians as John the Baptist. Whether Jesus was a follower of John before he began to preach; whether they even ever met is unknown.

There are some interesting conjectures by scholars as to why John was brought into the Jesus story. It is a historical fact that the Baptizer was a Jewish revivalist preacher who urged repentance on his fellow Jews because he felt the world was soon coming to an end. It is also a historical fact that the Baptizer was an object of suspicion to the Roman authorities because he was a persuasive preacher and had gathered a large following. That always meant the possibility of an uprising. And it is a final historical fact that John was put to death by Herod Antipas. (An estimated date of 28 c.e. is given by the modern scholar H. J. Schoepps.)

In his *Antiquities*, chapter 18, the historian Josephus reports:

". . . for Herod had John killed though he was a good man and commanded the Jews to exercise virtue through justice to one another and piety towards God. And by so doing to accept immersion, for immersion would be acceptable to God, not to expiate sin, but for the purification of the body after the soul was purified by righteousness.

"Greatly moved by hearing his words, many crowded around him. Herod who feared lest John's great influence over the people might lead them to revolt — for the people seemed likely to do anything he counseled — thought it best, by putting him to death, to prevent any mischief he might engender."

We note that John's "immersion" was a specific Jewish ritual, "not to expiate sin" as the Christian doctrine of baptism intends and as the gospels would have us believe (cf. Luke 1:77).

Why it has been asked, did Mark include in his gospel the Jewish revivalist preacher who was martyred before Jesus began his own ministry? Scholars have surmised that Jesus was not well-known when Mark wrote. John on the other hand still had a large following. To give Jesus more stature, it would be best to have the Baptizer placed in a subordinate role, they speculated.

We read how Mark has John proclaim, "After me comes one whose shoe latchets I am unworthy to untie. I baptized you with water; he will baptize you in the Holy Spirit." Mark even has John dressed in a hairy coat and wearing a leather girdle in imitation of Elijah the Hebrew prophet of the ninth century B.C.E. (2 Kings 1:8) (In Jewish tradition, Elijah was described as the forerunner of the messiah.)

We are thus presented with the odd situation in which a Jewish revivalist who died before Jesus, who had never heard of the crucifixion, certainly not of Christianity, now snugly installed as a Christian saint with churches and children named after him!

Scholars have suggested that Jesus may have listened to the Baptizer among the crowds that followed him; that he took up his cause when he was martyred and that he too began to preach repentance and the end of the world like John.

In that case, he would surely be on the "hit" list of the Roman authorities ever watchful for sedition. They might have informants among the Saducees.

MARK

Mark, writing about the year 75 was not a learned or especially literary person, say his critics. The King James translation was an improvement over his own style.

He tells us that after Jesus' immersion, he went off to the wilderness. There he spent forty days and nights tempted by Satan. We recall that Moses spent forty days and nights with God (Exodus 24:18).

When Jesus returned, he performed miracles; he stilled a storm, walked on water, fed a crowd with a few loaves and fishes. Most often, he healed the sick and cast out demons.

On a high mountain where he went with James, Peter and John, he talked with Moses and Elijah. The voice of God spoke to him and his face and garment became dazzlingly white (transfiguration). Here we see again the parallel Mark wishes to draw between Jesus and Moses. Moses' face becomes radiant after he talks with God on Mt. Sinai (Exodus 34:29).

Mark's intention in his gospel is to present the human life of an eternal being, a metaphysical being who is superior to Moses, to Judaism and to the Temple; who predicts his own death three times. Mark has Jesus put to death not by the "friendly" Romans but by the implacable Jews. In Mark, the Christ-killer theme takes its earliest form.

But Mark makes a number of "theologic" errors which the other evangelists have to correct: for example, he has a human like John the Baptizer baptize him. This "gaffe," produced much debate and many writings. The argument that Jesus was born human and became divine only after baptism, a theory called "adoptionism" occupied theologians for centuries. There existed a sect in Spain which adhered to this view and was denounced as heretical, as late as the eighth and ninth centuries.

Mark has Jesus cite two as the most important commandments,

of which the first is the Shema, the Jew's confession of faith, "Hear O Israel, the Lord our God is one God." This clearly would never do for a religion which deified Jesus. The citation does not appear in the three other gospels. Perhaps the other evangelists omitted it or it was edited out by later church writers.

Mark also has Jesus reply to one who calls him "good master," "Why do you call me good? Only God is good." Luke repeats it but not the other two.

And when Mark records Jesus' expiring cry, the first line from Psalm 22, "My God, my God, why hast thou forsaken me?" only Matthew repeats it. The other two, Luke and John substitute loftier, less "human" words.

Mark's gospel suggests that he has little love for the Jewish-Christians of his own day. He transfers his current antipathy to Jesus' time. Peter (dead about a decade when Mark writes) was an original member of the Jerusalem assembly of Jews who believed that Jesus was a messiah who would return. He gets some unfriendly treatment from Mark. So do the other Jewish disciples.

For example, while Jesus is suffering in the little garden enclosure called Gethsemane, anticipating his arrest and death, he tells his disciples "My heart is ready to break with grief. Stop here and stay awake." Jesus goes off to pray that the hour might pass him by and that the cup be taken from him, then he resigns himself to God's will. When he comes back, he finds the disciples fast asleep. "Asleep, Simon?" he says to Peter. "Were you not able to keep awake for one hour?" He tells them, "Stay awake, all of you and pray you be spared the test. The spirit is willing but the flesh is weak." Once more, he goes off to pray. When he returns they are again asleep.

Before this, Jesus has said that the disciples and Peter would disown him. They protest. Jesus says Peter will deny him three times before the cock crows twice. When he is arrested the disciples do desert him. Peter returns and does deny knowing him on three occasions as Jesus prophesied. Here Mark presents all the (Jewish) disciples as being cowardly.

An item which has puzzled some scholars is the kiss of Judas. Why, they ask, did Judas have to identify him thus? Was Jesus so unknown? They also comment on the use of the term rabbi. Apparently this word did not come into usage until some decades after Jesus' death.

What is interesting and more significant is Mark's derogation of Peter and the Jewish-Christian disciples. His hostility to Jews in general is marked, especially in the crucifixion drama. Nevertheless, Peter is shown by all the evangelists as being close to Jesus. This may be due to later editing when it was agreed that Peter would be needed as the primary figure for future apostolic successions.

MATTHEW

Matthew writing a decade or more after Mark is chiefly interested in a sound church administration. He appears to be more acute than Mark.

His gospel contains at least half of Mark and some of Luke. Whether he copied from Luke or vice versa or whether both drew on another source is a matter of interest only to scholars in this area.

Matthew is keenly aware that Peter has to play an important role in a church which is to be structured around Jesus. He therefore has to rescue him from Mark's scorn and to rehabilitate him. While he includes some of Mark's derogatory material, he has Jesus call Peter the rock (petra) on which the church is to be built. Of all the evangelists only Matthew has Jesus give Peter the "keys to the kingdom."

The gospels were edited and re-edited over a period of several hundred years not achieving their final form until the fourth century. Jesus' words to Peter, as reported by Matthew would provide irrefutable authorization that the successors of Peter, the bishops and later the Popes could use the power implied in the phrase "what you forbid on earth will be forbidden in Heaven and what you allow on earth will be allowed in Heaven."

Matthew was thought to be a converted Jew for a number of reasons, one of which was his copious use of the Scriptures — scholars have counted ninety citations. A minority of scholars do not agree.

Matthew describes Mary as a virgin, citing the Greek translation of the Hebrew for maiden, given as parthenon or virgin.

For this attribution of virginity, Matthew had many precedents in pagan folk history. Virginity was ascribed to mothers of heroes, emperors and gods. But it was the divinity of the father which had greater importance, it seems. Plato was regarded by some writers as having been fathered by Apollo.

When the second century church writer Justin Martyr was confronted with the many cases of virgin births and divine fatherhood, he retorted that Satan, having anticipated Christianity, imitated it in advance!

Matthew has Jesus born in Bethlehem to "fulfill Scriptures" as he says. The Scripture he has in mind is the passage in Micah (5:2) in which that prophet, writing some seven hundred years earlier prophesied that out of the little town of Bethlehem would come a ruler of Israel who would deliver the peoples from the Assyrian foe. Matthew ignores the Assyrians of whom Micah wrote and concentrates on the "ruler of Israel."

The gospelist Luke follows suit (or maybe it was vice versa) but the other two evangelists do not mention Jesus' birth at all.

Matthew also related that Herod, fearing that a "ruler of Israel" is to be born, sends his astrologers (Magi) to find out where the newborn is so he can put him to death. The magi do find out where he is but withhold this information from the wicked Herod. Enraged, Herod orders a "massacre of the innocents" in imitation presumably of Pharaoh (Exodus 1:16). An angel warns Joseph and he flees to Egypt. This, Matthew explains is to "fulfill Scripture" (Hosea 11:1). "Out of Egypt I have called my son."

The traditional Hebrew text says "I fell in love with Israel when he was still a child; And I have called him my son ever since Egypt." Is this ignorance or distortion?

Not content with this, Matthew even includes Jeremiah (31:15) of the seventh century B.C.E., in which we hear the echo of Rachel weeping for her children to "fulfill Scripture" in Herod's slaughter of the innocents:

To continue: After a number of angelic warnings and dreams, Joseph does not return to Judea but goes to Galilee to settle in a town called Nazareth to "fulfill Scripture" that "He shall be called a Nazarene."

On this point, scholars have raised some questions. If Matthew is referring to that verse in Scripture, namely Judges (13:5), he would mean, not a Nazarene but a Nazirite. A Nazirite is one dedicated to piety who uses no razor nor drinks any wine. Scholars have further pondered the question as to why no map of Jesus' time shows any town named Nazareth. Perhaps this will be explored in time. It is of only superficial concern to us here.

Both Matthew and Luke provide a genealogy for Jesus, tracing his Davidic descent. This would seem to contradict his divine birth but explanations, if there are any, might confuse the matter more.

Matthew divides his gospel into five parts, perhaps in imitation of the five books of Moses. He gives us the Sermon on the Mount (like Sinai?) and has four sections on teachings, parables and instructions to missionaries.

The Beatitudes which he has Jesus pronounce are says Dr. Sandmel:

> "justly famous as a splendid coherent expression of religious feeling. Each individual beatitude is paralleled in Biblical or rabbinic writing and can be considered as characteristic expressions of Jewish piety. A Jew finds himself on familiar territory when he reads the New Testament."

Christian scholars who have made a careful study of the Sermon report that it is skillful compilation of Psalms, Proverbs, Shemoneh Esra, Ecclesiasticus and other Jewish writings. They find the "Lord's Prayer" to be an amalgam of Jewish prayers from Talmud ending with the phrase, "deliver us from evil." The last phrase, "for thine is the glory, the power, etc." appears to be a later addition.

In setting down what he calls the new law of Christ, Matthew has chosen seven items which scholars have called a travesty of Judaism, laws which Jesus would not recognize. He also has Jesus say that an adulterous thought or murderous wish are equivalent to adultery and murder. He finds that the complete honesty enjoined in oaths not enough; he forbids oath at all. He advises loving your enemy, turning the other cheek, not resisting evil and giving your coat to one who sues you for your suit. In addition, he says that Jews have been taught to hate their enemy.

The idealistic precepts which Matthew puts into Jesus' mouth may have inspired some idealists and may even have been put into practice on occasion. But Jewish wisdom, knowing that man is imperfect does not expect perfection, only the effort to do as well as possible. Repentance and a contrite heart is as much as can be expected of man who can never be perfect as God is perfect.

As for the thoroughly dishonest statement that Jews are taught to hate their enemies, there is not a word anywhere in the vast literature of Judaism which indicates this. Concern for one's enemy rather may be found in many parts of rabbinic literature.

The harsh injunction (Matthew 5:29 ff) which advises:

> "If your right hand is your undoing, cut it off and fling it away; it is better to lose one part of your body than that the whole of it go to hell,"

makes one wonder whether that third century ascetic and learned church writer, the work-obsessed Origen, did not have this in mind when he castrated himself.

From his gospel, we get the impression that Matthew's chief interest was a well-functioning, sound and stable church. His instructions, his handbook for missionaries, his orderliness suggests the capable administrator.

But his portrait of Jesus is not a pretty one; it appears to be his own. Those heated words he puts in Jesus' mouth are incomprehensible in a person he wishes to present as divine. "Were those words actually said by Jesus," remarks Dr. Sandmel, "they would make him out a harsh, unbelievable and altogether frail human."

Matthew diminishes the one he wished to elevate when he has Jesus address his fellow Jews with these words:

> "You murderers of the prophets (a vastly overworked slogan) blind to the deeper truths, whitewashed tombs concealing bones and filth . . . fair outside but full of crime and hypocrisy . . . you snakes, you vipers' broods, how can you escape being condemned to hell. I send you prophets, sages, teachers; some of them you will kill and

crucify ... on you will fall the guilt of all the innocent blood spilt on the ground." (Matthew 23)

With these words, the blood of Jesus' own descendants flowed in rivers and streams over the years and the centuries. Did Jesus really say these words? (In his account of the crucifixion as we saw, Matthew was even more malevolent.)

LUKE

Luke a Gentile, writing at the end of the first century or early in the second is also anti-Judaic. (All the gospels had to be anti-Judaic to make a place for their own belief.)

Had Luke lived today, he might have been a successful writer of fiction. He is inventive, creative, lively and fanciful. He has been described as an artist rather than as a reporter or historian.

Luke's aim was to present Christianity as the continuation and culmination of Judaism — with Christian improvements.

Early on in his gospel, we observe his inventiveness. He creates a set of parents for John the Baptizer. He calls the father-to-be of the Baptizer, Zechariah, and makes him a priest. The mother is named Elizabeth (Elisheba in Hebrew) and she is also of priestly descent. (Did not some second century chronicler endow Jesus with maternal grandparents and did not the church dutifully make saints of these two, named Anne and Joachim?)

Luke's Zechariah at his prayers is told by the angel Gabriel that his wife, though past child bearing will nevertheless conceive and bear a son whom he is to name Jokhanan (John). Whereupon, Zechariah is struck dumb. Six months later, Gabriel visits Mary in Nazareth and tells her she will also conceive a child to be named Jesus. His father will be the Holy Spirit.

Mary now visits Elizabeth whom Luke makes her kinswoman. As she enters, the foetus in Elizabeth's womb leaps up. Luke may intend this to signify joy or perhaps to acknowledge John's future obeisant role.

When the Baptizer is born, the gospelist introduces some dramatic tension. The relatives want to name the baby Zechariah after the father. Readers of the gospel know this is impossible because the baby is to be the future Baptizer. In agreement with his wife, Zechariah indicates he wants the baby to be called "John." At once his speech is restored.

John grows up and takes the role assigned to him. To show that John is offering Christian baptism, Luke has John offer it to a Pharisee who refuses. This device of Luke's "proves" John is a bona fide Christian.

Each of the evangelists in his own way makes use of the Baptizer, who is always emphasizing his subordinate role, always deprecating his own worth compared to that of Jesus. Throughout the gospels, we see how subtly John has been slipped into Christian religious history.

Luke's birth legends are more poetic than Matthew's. There is a little clumsiness at first when he apparently has Joseph lead the heavily pregnant Mary from Nazareth to Bethlehem so Jesus can be born there "to fulfill Scripture." Luke's device is a census-taking which requires that each person be registered from his home town. For this purpose, Luke pretends that Joseph is a native of Bethlehem. He makes up for this awkwardness by the fanciful story of angels leading the shepherd to the stable (no room at the inn) where the newborn "deliverer" or savior is lying in a manger. There have always been folk tales about heroes and demi-gods or gods being born in caves or other humble places in contrast to their future glorified status.

Luke's story of the nativity has inspired many lovely songs and stories. The peaceful animals, the awestruck shepherds, the chorus of angels, these have delighted many a child at Christmas.

Luke maintains his Jewish orientation while making it clear that Jews will be rejected by God if they reject Jesus.

He includes a circumcision for the Baptizer. Similarly he includes one for Jesus. To celebrate this, the Catholic church has had a Feast of the Circumcision on their calendar for years. Then, perhaps to distance the church from this Jewish rite, they renamed it the Feast of the Octave. More recently, its origin has been further obscured by its present name, The Feast of the Solemnity of our Lady, Mother of God.

Luke went so far in his "Jewishness" as to include the ceremony of the ransoming of the first born male by a token payment. This pidyon ha ben is celebrated by observant Jews to this very day.

Luke enlivens his gospel by introducing one Simeon, an old man who has been awaiting the birth of Jesus. Now, having seen the "Lord's Messiah" as Luke puts it, he can die happy. (In this Luke seems to copy the patriarch Isaac who also can die happy having seen his son Joseph (Gen. 46:30)) Simeon prophesies that Jesus the babe will grow up to be a deliverer and a "light to the nations." Here Luke calls on passages in Genesis and Isaiah.

Luke has also given one line to a prophetess Anna who predicts the greatness of Jesus. Now, having had them recite their lines, Luke drops them both.

Of all the evangelists, only Luke writes about the twelve-year-old Jesus whose parents forget about him and return home. After a days' journey, they notice his absence and return to the Temple. There, they find him in grave discourse with teachers and doctors of law.

"Why did you search?" asks the twelve-year-old. "Did you not know I was bound to be in my <u>Father's</u> house? Luke makes his point.

Luke is the only evangelist who tells the story about a good Samaritan who stops to help a man who was robbed and beaten. Two Temple functionaries a priest and a Levite ignore the man but a "second class" Jew, a Samaritan, does help.

ACTS

"Acts of the Apostles," Luke's sequel to his gospel has been called a quasi-history by those who believe there are some nuggets of history in this essentially meager book of forty pages. It is full of myth, legend, fanciful tales and literary invention. Some scholars reject it unconditionally as history. Fundamentalists accept it whole. Most liberal scholars agree it is unreliable.

Written in the early or mid-part of the second century when both Peter and Paul were long dead, the author creates actions and speeches for them to suit his missionary purposes.

The author of "Acts" knew how important it was for the Jewish origins of the nascent church to be retained. The claim to legitimacy required the solid base of Judaism, the religion of Jesus, Peter, Paul and other apostles. The Jewish Scripture provided the source from which the Church would extract its validation.

The gaggle of assemblies, later to be organized into an orthodox structure barely existed until Paul's vigorous missionizing.
These assemblies would follow Paul's metaphysical ideas; some
would wish to discard Judaism altogether. Leaders who determined by the end of the second century which gospels should be
included, knew that the gnostic, spiritual sects would eventually
be dissipated. But they could not discard Paul and his embryonic
Christology; this after all, would be the foundation of Christianity, separating it finally from the parent religion.

In "Acts," Luke presents us with a so-called history of the
years 33–63 approximately. This is assumed to be the period from
Jesus' death and resurrection until Paul settles in Rome. (Note
that Luke is writing about a century or so <u>after</u> the events he
depicts.)

He takes on himself the task of juggling the disparate and
often conflicting ideas that prevailed at the time he actually
wrote. He wishes to present the Church as if it were and had
always been a unified and harmonious whole. To this end, he
does not hesitate to supply from his imagination whatever will
serve that purpose. In addition to the obligatory vilification of
Jews, he offers myths, legends and artistic literary vignettes.

Such obviously fictional tales with which Luke entertains us
like that of Ananias and Sapphira who both drop dead because
they lied about the money they could contribute, or that of Judas
whose belly splits open on the very ground he bought with his
tainted pieces of silver (In Matthew, Judas returns the money and
hangs himself), these we shall not consider. We shall mention
only those stories which are regarded seriously and even quoted
by reputable and respectable church writers.

For example, Luke puts Paul in Judea so he can be present
when the "stoning of Stephen" takes place. There seems to be
nothing to substantiate this.

Luke gives us the dramatic "Road to Damascus" romance
when Paul, blinded and in a trance, has a dialogue with Jesus who
reproaches him for persecuting him. After three days, he is
healed by one, Ananias, who is told by God in a vision to lay
hands on Saul/Paul. Paul is cured, baptized and thereafter
becomes an ardent missionary. From Paul's letter to the Galatians,

we learn nothing of such a stupendous happening. Knowing Paul as we do, we can be sure he would have proclaimed it to all.

In Galatians 1:16–17, he says, in support of his claim to be an apostle, "God chose to reveal his son to me." Then he tells how he went to Araby (desert?) perhaps to meditate and then returned to Damascus. That is all.

But Luke's ingenious mind seized on the word Damascus and created a story of it, his fanciful "Road to Damascus" narrative. If Paul had indeed had a trance, been blinded, baptized and converted after talking with Jesus, I am sure we would have heard of it from him. He was always having to show his credentials (2 Cor. 12). What better proof could he have to give his listeners of his right to be an apostle!

Luke writing his "Acts" more than half a century after Paul, could draw on Paul's letters for clues, then use his imagination to compose a "history." He does the same thing when he concocts the "stoning of Stephen" story as we shall see later.

As for Paul's Roman citizenship, some scholars doubt this. They declare that Luke, not Rome conferred this honor on Paul. Roman citizenship was not bestowed very often on non-Romans especially not those of humble birth, poverty and obscurity like Paul. Had Paul by chance inherited this honor from some illustrious forebear, we should have heard it, not from Luke alone but from Paul who would have proclaimed it widely.

It has been thought that Luke used this as a device to extricate Paul from some of his missionary misadventures. Also it seems to have been used to legitimate a supposed appeal Paul made to the Roman emperor against his Jewish opponents. Perhaps this was also the pretext for getting Paul to Rome. (Here he conveniently dies according to legend so the Church at Rome can claim him along with Peter.)

Luke tells us that Paul was allowed to lodge there by himself (under the guard of a Roman soldier) and preach. But we never do learn whether he got that hearing from the emperor, a privilege granted to Roman citizens. One notes also that Paul is beheaded not crucified as is Peter who is not a Roman citizen. The writer of that legend in the second century knew that Roman citizens were spared crucifixion. The legend that both

Peter and Paul died on the same day is rather more than most scholars can ingest. But at the time of the legend, it may have helped strengthen the claim of the already strong Roman church, later to become the seat of the papacy.

Luke tells us that Paul delivered a splendid speech before the learned Athenians on Mars Hill (Areopagus). Luke has Paul observe an altar with an inscription "To an Unknown God." From these words, he launches into a speech about the creator God who is not an idol but the father of all, who commands men to repent and who has sent a man of his choosing, raising him from the dead to give this message.

At these words about resurrection, the Athenians scoff and go off. Yet all we read in Paul of this presumed speech is a phrase (1 Cor. 1:24) that to the Greeks, his ideas are foolishness.

That Paul ever delivered a speech to the Athenians is doubtful. If he did, it would obviously not be the one recorded in Acts.

The learned Dutch humanist, Erasmus, writing in his (1515) book *In Praise of Folly* takes Paul to task for Luke's words.

> "Indeed," he says, "St. Paul minces and mangles some citations and seems to wrest them to a different sense from that for which they were intended. It was not 'to an unknown god' which was inscribed on the altar. The whole phrase reads, 'to the gods of Asia, Africa and Europe and to all foreign and unknown gods.'"

Leaving aside Luke's stories and misrepresentations, we see that his chief purpose in "Acts" is to present the Church as a united and harmonious whole. The facts, however, are quite otherwise as any Christian scholar will confirm.

The Jewish assembly in Jerusalem with Peter and James were at odds with Paul and his Gentile mission. Luke tries to gloss over these differences.

He gives Paul a Jewish name, Saul and he makes him a student under Gamaliel in Jerusalem. He even has him recite a speech in Hebrew. There is no indication that Paul knew any Hebrew. His language was Greek and his Bible the Septuagint.

Some scholars do not believe that Luke gave Paul the real

distinction he merited as the pre-eminent missionary of the new church. Dr. Sandmel suggests that Luke may have wanted to downplay Paul; his undisciplined spirituality would not make for an orderly Jewish-oriented church such as Luke wanted.

PETER

It was Peter who needed to be elevated in this hyphenated church. Peter, the Jewish-Christian, had to be shown as "pro-Gentile" to indicate unity. Luke therefore has Peter tell of a thrice-repeated vision in which Peter is told he may abandon the Jewish dietary laws!

To raise him up from the bumbling craven he is made to appear in Mark, Luke has this unlettered fisherman deliver eloquent, erudite speeches. He has him heal and perform miracles. In short, he is presented as a worthy disciple of Jesus and a worthy head of the unified church which is to be. (The New Testament letters called First and Second Peter were composed many years after the genuine Peter died.)

STEPHEN

Before leaving Acts, a few words about Stephen are necessary. I think Luke invented him.

We come across Stephen in the year of Jesus' death or shortly thereafter. In Acts, chapters 6 and 7, he is described as a man of grace and power with a face like an angel. Although he has been appointed, along with six other Hellenist Jews to work as a simple deacon, he is shortly working signs and miracles.

Stephen has been called before the council of the Jerusalem assembly to answer charges that he has been speaking against the law of Moses, saying Jesus would alter it.

In fifty tedious verses, Stephen relates the history of the Jews from Abraham to Moses. God did not give the law to Moses, says Stephen. The people spurned him and built a golden calf. When Solomon built a house for God (the Temple presumably) God spurned that too for God does not live in houses built by men. He quotes Isaiah 66:1: "Heaven is my throne and the earth my footstool."

When Stephen finishes this dull summary, suddenly without transition, he upbraids the council uttering the famous slogan (which did not come into use until <u>after</u> Stephen's supposed speech) about Jews slaying their prophets, including the Righteous One whom they have betrayed and murdered. Here again Luke is the ventriloquist and Stephen the dummy, the mouthpiece for delivering lines. Since Stephen is supposed to be delivering his speech around the year 33 or 34 (perhaps) there were only Jewish followers of Jesus. Perhaps some Gentile godfearers were part of the little sect. Paul had not yet formulated his thesis.

The Jews, says Stephen, received the law from angels not Moses and besides they did not keep it. Then he quotes from Ezekiel about the heavens opening; then he quotes Daniel about seeing the son of Man standing at the right hand of God.

So far, he seems to have said nothing that could be construed as blasphemous. But Luke has the outraged council, grinding their teeth in rage, lunge at him with one accord.

Note however that each one of them first lays his coat at the feet of none other than Saul/Paul.

Then they take him outside the walls for stoning. The saintly Stephen forgives them and dies peacefully.

The story seems totally contrived. Luke makes Stephen a Hellenist Jew along with six other Greeks who are elected deacons. Stephen parrots Paul's words about secondary angels giving the law. He talks anachronistically about Jews always slaying their prophets including the last one, Jesus. In the year 33–34 during which time this incident is supposed to take place, there were just a small group of devout Jews who believed Jesus was the messiah they were looking for. Perhaps there were some Gentile godfearers along. But that was all. We begin to hear from Paul only between 50 and 60. The whole Pentecostal scene appears to be a literary device to get his story started. If Luke is writing a century after the supposed event, who will be around to gainsay him?

But Luke seems determined to get the Hellenists (the future base of the new Church) into his account and he wants to segue into the story of Paul, the Hellenist Jew. Stephen provides a good transition; Paul acquiesces to the so-called stoning; he is an unbeliever; he gets dramatically converted and the second half of "Acts" deals with his missionary deeds. These make a nice contrast to his former hard-hearted stance.

Stephen, we note, appears this one and only time. He recites his piece and is gone. Luke has no further use for him.

Luke now recapitulates Paul's missionary adventures including some probable facts among the fanciful tales of escape. At the end, via the device stated above, he drops him off in Rome, there to be martyred as the legends report.

In my comments on the synoptic gospels, I tried to extract some of the basic themes as I understood them.

Looking again at those Jewish-Christians, the original followers of Jesus, we see that the loss of an admired leader must have been deeply painful to them. The nature of his death and the failure of his mission must have also caused them disappointment and sorrow. Whether they had regarded him as a warrior-messiah or whether he so regarded himself is not certain. Certain it is that he had not behaved like a messiah; he had not vanquished the oppressing Romans; he had not initiated the new world in which every day would be as a joyful Sabbath, a kingdom of God on earth. Instead he had been put to death ignobly as a seditionist.

Though the wicked world had not given way to a better one, some of his followers wished to believe it still would. A rumor spread that he had been seen in Emmaus and in Galilee, alive.

Paul, as we know, was strangely affected by the rumor. A troubled Hellenist Jew, he developed ideas which were acceptable to those Gentiles flocking to Judaism, but were alien to Palestinian Jews.

As for Peter, he appears to have taken his departure from the Jewish-Christian scene after the death of James, Jesus' brother and leader of the Jerusalem assembly.

We read in Josephus, Chapter 20, that an arrogant Sadducee priest, Ananus, illegally put James to death by ordering him stoned. The others, presumably Pharisees, were outraged and complained to Agrippa who ordered the young priest removed from office.

One may speculate that Peter returned to traditional Judaism after this event. Recalling the bitterness between him and Paul (Galatians 2:11ff) we know Peter did not share Paul's frantic need to abrogate the Mosaic law. Peter might prefer the sanctuary of his thousand-year-old Judaism to the alien ambiance of Paul's Gentile Christianity.

The new Christ idea of vicarious atonement, initiated by Paul, the development of this idea by the evangelist John, and the support supplied by the gospels of Mark, Matthew and Luke, all formed the base for the new religion.

Jesus had been drafted by Paul into what later became Christianity; John the Baptizer had been slipped into Christian history; Peter the humble follower was groomed by Matthew and Luke in their gospels, for a special role as Jesus' primary disciple. From him the apostolic succession would proceed.

Tradition and legend has it that both Peter and Paul died at Rome as we have said. Peter was crucified upside down, according to legend, presumably in deference to Jesus. Paul was said to have been beheaded there.

The church at Rome was thus blessed with two martyrs. Being moreover a rich church and a stronghold of orthodoxy, it would achieve primacy. Bishops and then popes would head the church with Peter as chief saint. Paul had a basilica outside the walls.

"By the year 250," says Paul Johnson in his *History of Christianity*, Rome was rich enough to support a bishop, forty-six presbyters, seven deacons, seven sub-deacons, forty-two acolytes and fifty-two exorcists, readers and doorkeepers." He notes that the church had a charity list of over 1,500 and vast quantities of goods, gold and silver plates.

The church at St. Peter, that imposing basilica was built and rebuilt over the spot where Peter's bones were reputed to be buried.

JOHN

The Fourth Gospel has been called the spiritual gospel. It has also been called an essay on Christian supernaturalism. John seems very little interested in the historical Jesus. Though he relates some incidents and events, he focuses on the Logos that aspect of God, known to him as the Christ.

This was an aspect of God, known briefly to man as Jesus the incarnated one who carried out that function ideated by Paul of serving as a sacrificial atonement for man's sins.

When John presents Jesus Christ as the divine son of God, as the Word made flesh, he had gone much farther than Paul intended. The Jew Paul saw Jesus as the <u>kyrios,</u> the lord and master but never as God. He was an emanation, a kind of God-power but never God.

It is true that Paul's monotheism seemed to be showing some dilution; he lacked the rugged religious convictions of his Hebraic prophet forebears. Weakened perhaps by the Hellenist environment and by his own personal problems, passive Paul sought an advocate, an intermediary. When he introduced his idea of Jesus as a kind of whipping boy for himself, he did not expect that almost a century later, John would use Jesus for <u>his</u> own needs. His needs were different from Paul's.

John, a Gentile had not experienced Torah, nor a thousand-year-old single God. Product of an apocalyptic, eschatologic environment, he was one of that fraternity of thinkers who long to grasp the unreachable, to sense the unknowable. They always exist; they exist today. He thought he found the means in Paul's Christ. Paul had opened the path; John extended it and gave it the direction he wished it to take. His reading of Hebrew Scripture (Septúagint) to which the figure of Jesus was attached, was alien to rabbinic Judaism. They opposed him, that small number of rabbis and scribes. (It should be noted that the rest of Judaism was not especially interested in the squabbling which went on.)

In the Christ idea, John evidently found something he could relate to, personally. It represented for him the pure spiritual principle which led to the mystery of God and to a knowledge of "ultimate reality." The Jews denied this ineffable truth which John had discovered for himself. Jews were therefore unspiritual, material, worldly, carnal and "sons of darkness" as against the "sons of light" represented by believers in Christ.

John's Christ has very little connection with the Jesus of the other gospelists. Here are no birth legends, no baptism, no anguish in Gethsemane, no loud expiring cry. John's Christ is removed from things human. He is divine; he is in control of his destiny. When he dies, John has him say "It is done" quite calmly. In this gospel, we hear only John talking; the voice of the synoptic Jesus is barely audible.

There are those traditional theologians who wish to believe that the John of this gospel is actually Jesus' Jewish disciple. But this seems to be highly doubtful. No Jew, for example, could possibly say: "Whoever eats my flesh and drinks my blood possesses eternal life. My flesh is real food; my blood is real drink." In almost every book of Torah, the eating of blood is prohibited, considered an abomination. (Also, John, were he Jesus' disciple, would have to be almost if not actually a centenarian. The gospel was written 100 c.e., maybe later.)

Most conclusive, I believe, is the way John thinks. He would be classed as a Gentile Christian, speaking in Greek, to a young already Christian church of his time. His fury against the Jews who do not acknowledge his God is intemperate. He rails against them as the actual crucifiers of Jesus. (Pilate just could not stand up to the "Jews" threats and importuning.) We note that he uses the term "Jews" in a pejorative way, no less than sixty times. "It is as if," says Dr. Eckardt, "one would say of President Kennedy that he had been assassinated by an American."

John teaches that the Jews are an apostate fallen people, demonic actually, who wish to murder the true God in the person of his son. He puts into Jesus' mouth these words to his brethren":

> "You are of your Father, the Devil. And the lusts of your Father you will do. He was a murderer from the beginning. He abode not in the truth because there was no truth in him. . ."

"In its utility for later Jew-haters," says scholar Dr. Sandmel, "the Fourth gospel is pre-eminent among New Testament writings."

We may perhaps understand the immoderate rage of a frustrated missionary of two thousand years ago. Less understandable is the Church's stance in keeping as "sacred" those hate-filled words.

I am told that his gospel is a favorite among clergymen. One modern scholar does admit somewhat ruefully that the evangelist may have been responsible for bringing into the church a "one-sided and self-centered mysticism. He makes no mention in his report of the gospel's all pervasive anti-Judaism.

John's Christ, eternal and pre-existent is God in the temporary human form of the Jewish preacher, Jesus. Later church apologists went further. They described Christ as the "very Godness of God" according to Dr. Sandmel who explains the process which led to the doctrine of the Trinity.

What a contrast we find here between John's Christ and the Jesus of the first gospelist. In Mark 12:29, we read Jesus' words when he is asked which is the first of all the commandments. "Hear, O Israel," Jesus replies, "the Lord our God is the one God."

In the Fourth gospel, there is included an addendum, chapter 21. This clumsily written section has the resurrected Jesus dine with his disciples on freshly caught and broiled fish. He then authorizes Peter to head the Church. He also indicates Peter's death by crucifixion. (No one knows how Peter died half a century or so before this gospel was set down.) A martyr's death would however add to the lustre and glory of the Church.

We might note here that Paul the Jew never attributed divinity to Jesus. But his concept that Jesus' death expiated sin—the resurrection was the proof—formed the base on which the evangelists built their gospels.

When the Fourth gospel was written in the second century, no one any longer expected that the world would end and the messianic age begin. John has Jesus return to heaven whence he came. Now the "Holy Spirit" would act as intermediary for man.

To Christian believers in the Trinity, God has a component nature. For a Jew, this must forever be an alien concept since he sees God as indivisible. John describes a being who appears to be God. Except that he calls him Christ.

Before leaving the chapter a few words about that strange and obscure book called "Revelation" may be useful.

It is part of the apocalyptic literature which abounded during the first and second centuries, having begun as far back at least as the Jewish Book of Daniel in 165 B.C.E. A book of ecstatic visions which drew heavily on the library of Jewish writings, "Revelation" was circulated for the use of Christians who were suffering from Roman persecutions at the end of the first Christian century.

In enigmatic words and visions, the author who calls himself John of Patmos—he is not related to the evangelist—writes to encourage the faithful to believe in ultimate vindication and triumph over their present trials.

Without attempting any discussion of the mostly obscure references whose symbolism is now unclear, we note that "Revelation" has provided us with some titles of books and films such as the *Four Horsemen of the Apocalypse,* the *Seventh Seal,* the *Grapes of Wrath* and probably others.

For a long time, the church leaders were reluctant to include this visionary work in their canon just as Jewish religious leaders were uncertain about the Book of Daniel (from which Revelation draws material). But they capitulated, deciding it was better to have one book marked acceptable in order to discourage the many others.

"Revelation" has provided many an evangelical and table-thumping preacher with matter for lively if mystifying sermons.

VI

ANTI-JUDAISM AS
CHURCH THEOLOGY

"Christianity means antisemitism." Professor Eckardt may have surprised some of his co-religionists when he pronounced those words in a 1974 Baylor University symposium on Jewish-Christian relations.

But Jews were not surprised. It was a familiar fact.

That it was again so firmly expressed by this outstanding fighter against antisemitism was heartening to Jews.

Dr. James Parkes, the Anglican churchman, a pioneer writer in this area has told us for half a century that

> "Antisemitism from the first century to the twentieth century is a Christian creation and a Christian responsibility."

In his preface to a book by Alan T. Davies called *Antisemitism and the Foundations of Christianity,* Dr. Parkes says

> ". . . it is dishonest thenceforth to refuse to face the fact that the basic root of modern antisemitism lies squarely on the Gospels and the rest of the New Testament."

That honest churchmen should be profoundly disturbed by the indifferent mass killing of Jews in the Holocaust is not unexpected. That so many more were shocked and surprised tells us that they had never before given serious thought to the centuries-long persecutions of Jews simply because they were Jews.

The average lay Christian did not regard these acts as having any connection with himself. The previous reports he had read fleetingly about outrages, took no deep hold on his mind or heart. More often persecutions occurred in Europe to a people whom he had been taught to disdain or at best regard with indifference. With exceptions.

Some years ago, I was sitting for a portrait by a liberal intelligent artist. She was not a church-goer but she had been raised in a Protestant home.

I hung up my dripping coat; it was raining hard. "Bad weather," I said mechanically.

"Yes, isn't it dreadful," she agreed.

We talked desultorily of one thing or another. I mentioned a newspaper item I had read that morning about some figures on the Holocaust.

"Yes, wasn't that dreadful," she said. Her tone of voice was identical with the tone in which she had agreed about the weather.

In later years, I told myself she was busy working, not listening. But I knew it was not so. She was not really interested. Not she, nor most Christians. Some of their best friends were Jews however.

I offer here a capsule history for the many uninformed Christians and for the fewer but also uninformed Jews. This brief survey glances at the longest-lasting persecution of one religious group by another in the entire history of mankind.

With imperial power in church hands at the close of the fourth century, repressive civil and social legislation began. This legislation has been compared, not incorrectly, with the Nuremberg laws of Hitler's Germany. The Church laws were not so efficiently enforced as under Hitler so Jews could move and manage in this unsettled and shifting world of the early Christian era.

Large scale atrocities did not begin until the Crusades which lasted from the 12th to the 14th centuries. These "pilgrimages" were designed by Church and state leaders (kings, nobles, knights) to attack the growing Moslem power, to gather booty and conquer territory and thus also deal with the problem of unrest and excess population among the poor.

Jews early on became victims, losing life and property. The Crusaders themselves were slaughtered or killed off by disease as they attacked the Moslem forces in the East. At least a hundred thousand, probably more, Christians died.

Survivors brought back with them the bubonic plague. The plague killed an estimated one third of the population of Europe.

This Black Death was attributed to a conspiracy of Jews who were accused of poisoning the wells in order to exterminate their Christian oppressors. That Jews died along with Christians did not diminish the accusations. Perhaps Jewish deaths may have been somewhat fewer in proportion, some writer guessed, because of their religious rite of hand washing and ritual body cleansing. (The conspiracy idea will be discussed below.)

Crimes against Jews included, not only the common ones of robbery, looting, extortion and blackmail, but the more serious ones of book and synagogue burning, rape, forced mass conversion and the abduction of children to be brought up as Catholic. Accusations of desecration of the host (regarded as the body of Christ), accusations of ritual murder (killing a Christian child for blood for the Passover) were used to extract "confessions" by torture. These "confessions" justified their being burned at the stake or otherwise put to death.

(A case of "blood libel" actually occurred in Russia in 1913 but the victim, Mendel Beilis, was finally cleared through the efforts of world opinion. Beilis however was a broken man for the rest of his life.)

Expulsion was a popular method in the Middle Ages by means of which nobles and kings could confiscate Jewish property and cancel debts which were owed where Jews had been active as financial agents in the interests of kings and nobles. There is a letter extant dated 1349 from Charles IV of Bohemia to his friend the Margrave of Brandenburg promising him three Jewish houses "when the next massacre of Jews takes place."

Wherever and whenever Jews had been left in peace, they prospered. Their generally high level of civilization, their education, sobriety, chaste family life and their industrious habits brought them material gain. But their prosperity was also their misfortune.

The peasants, often semi-Christianized, illiterate and barbarous resented them. The lessons of the Church Fathers which had filtered down to them through priests and monks had taught them that Jews were an accursed deicide people destined to suffer misery and enslavement for not accepting Jesus as Savior. Inflamed often by ignorant and superstitious monks, they would fall upon the defenseless Jews to bring them to the state of misery prescribed for them by the Church Fathers.

During the barbarous Middle Ages—which for Jews lasted until well after Hitler's twentieth century—they were exposed to mob attacks; women were raped; whole communities were slain or burned alive; children were sold into slavery.

The ghetto was another form of persecution which church and state employed. The Church was always uneasy that contact with Jews might unsettle the faith of the still nominal Christians. It was a form of enslavement as well. When Jews did go out of the ghetto gates (which were locked at night) they were forced to wear a distinguishing "Jew badge," usually yellow, a conical hat and a covering garment which set them apart.

Mockery and contempt were encouraged. The Jew was caricatured in every medium: in plays, writings and in art. This use of contempt may have been the technique designed to minimize the superstitious fear of Jews. Peasants and others were themselves in perpetual fear of hell-fire, a terror forced on them by the all-powerful Church.

The Jew as devil had a powerful hold on the medieval mind. Not only the ignorant and superstitious peasant but all seemed thus affected. The 14th century has been termed the century of the devil.

This century was also the time when the conspiracy fantasy originated of a worldwide plan to exterminate Christians (Here we can see the terrified Christians projecting their own feelings on Jews). Conspiracy suggests that evil and menace lurk; that conspirators have some special knowledge.

Who could better fit this description than the "theological" Jew created by the Fourth gospelist. This imaginary creature, "son of darkness," had to be evil enough to kill the "true god," the "light of the world" as conceived in John's dualist-influenced mind.

We might mention here that when Isaiah (13:21) was castigating Israel and threatening the ruin of her homes where beasts and owls and ostriches and goat-demons would now live, the translators mistook the word "goat-demons" and turned it into "devil." The Revised edition remedied it to read "satyrs." For this reason we have a portrait of the devil, complete with horns, tail and cloven hoof. The image of the devil as goat has persisted.

The movie *Norma Rae* has an exchange between the union organizer from New York who has come to help the young woman get the exploited textile workers to join forces against the unfair tactics of management.

"You're a Jew, aren't you?" says Norma Rae.

"Yes," he replies.

"I thought Jews had horns and a tail,' she teases. They both laugh.

That colonial lady can better be understood. She sees her first Jew. She examines him, turning him around. "Thou'rt like any man," she says in candid surprise.

Or that mountain villager in Italy, father of a friend. He had gone to town to buy some clothing. Our friend related how his father, an intelligent and literate man, had expressed his surprise that the Jewish merchant was devoid of horn or tail. This was many years ago, of course. But the myth lingers on.

As for the conspiracy fantasy, it is still in force today, still being used for antisemitic purposes. Antisemitism is now called anti-Zionism but the words are often interchangeable.

For those readers who have heard about the hoax called the *Protocols of the Elders of Zion* but did not know exactly what it meant—as I did not—here is the story extracted from a number of sources:

The *Protocols* forgery began more than a hundred years ago. In 1868, a German post office worker, discredited for his part in a forgery scandal turned to novel writing under the name of Sir John Retcliffe instead of his own name Hermann Goedsche.

He wrote a fantastic antisemitic tale in which he had twelve men of the twelve tribes of Israel having their usual centennial meeting in a Jewish cemetery in Prague. Their plan to conquer the world is relayed to the devil who is naturally present. He will spread the news to worldwide Jewry to execute the strategies.

Then Goedsche found a satire called *Dialogue in Hell* published in 1864 written by a French lawyer Maurice Joly who deplored the politics of Napoleon III. He saw that he could plagiarize and use it. These dialogues, purporting to be between the shades of Montesquieu and Machiavelli, has Machiavelli justifying control of the press, repressive measures, financial maneuverings, relations with the Vatican and other presumably unsavory actions which Napoleon III is engaging in. Goedsche now reworded the *Dialogue* to pretend that Jews not Napoleon III, were planning these measures.

(Joly incidentally was fined 300 francs, given 15 months imprisonment and had his books confiscated for "action against the government.")

Goedsche turned his fiction into a presumably factual account in which he has a rabbi make a speech at a convocation of Jews in Lemberg, using all the *Dialogue* material to make it seem like a Jewish plan for world conquest.

Other antisemites used as a setting the actual meeting of Jews at the 1897 World Jewish Congress of Zionists who sought to find a haven from the pogroms and persecutions they were suffering from the actions of just such antisemites as Goedsche. By setting the supposed conspiracy meeting at an actual place (Basle, Switzerland) the antisemites gave the forgery an appearance of verisimilitude.

In any event there were enough professional antisemites who were glad to seize on anything they could use to scapegoat the hapless Jews.

The material came into the hands of a religious fanatic, a

Russian, Serge Nilus, who had written a pamphlet on the Anti-Christ. It was published in Russia and was used to foment anti-Jewish riots and pogroms at the time the Tsar's autocratic rule was crumbling.

The strategy of the *Protocols* was, and still is, a plan to incite hatred and fear of the "all powerful" menacing conspiracy of worldwide Jewry. It was used during the Dreyfus affair at the end of the nineteenth century; it was used in Russia; it was even used in the United States after the disorganization and fears following the first World War, but here, there was a strong opposition to this shocking hoax.

Hitler made maximum use of this forgery. It was disseminated almost all over the world, translated in every tongue. And in 1967, a new Arabic translation was made in Cairo after the Six-Day War.

The author, professor and clergyman, Dr. Franklin Littell, an active worker for Jewish-Christian friendship tells of a report that King Faisal of Saudi Arabia had had this forgery handsomely printed and bound, to present to his western guests!

This conspiracy hoax which was discovered by an English reporter stationed in Constantinople in 1921 (Istanbul since 1930) has been described as "ridiculous nonsense" by a Swiss judge, has been proved over and over to be utterly false, malicious and stupid, yet has continued to be kept alive like an evil jinni to be evoked wherever there is need to vilify innocent Jews.

In the case of the *Protocols* the intent was malign. In the case of a missionary who devoutly carries his New Testament with him, the intent is benign. Unfortunately his book contains malign matter in the crucifixion drama and in its vilification of Jews.

There are sections that can be helpful and inspiring. But to stamp all of it sacred must surely cast doubt on any part which may be.

I know that Protestant and Catholic religious educators have been working at an improved curriculum which, it is hoped, will minimize the anti-Judaism inherent in the New Testament. Would it not be simpler to delete those segments that require so much "interpretation." I doubt that their absence will be noted.

One evening at a public meeting, I asked the speaker just that question. I perceived an expression of near panic on his face. He did not answer but dismissed the question with a negating gesture of his hand.

To this rigidly indoctrinated Christian, I had said the unsayable.

In ironic contrast, was the experience I had at the Church of the Holy Sepulchre in Jerusalem.

Tourists in Israel, we all got off the bus which held mostly Christian pilgrims. We followed the guide to a cave-like structure, murky and ill-lighted where the tomb of Jesus was supposed to be.

I see the face of the Greek Orthodox priest. He was heavily bearded, I remember, and his priestly attire looked murky too. Perhaps it was the gloom in that small enclosure which made the visit seem conspiratorial. Perhaps it was that odd little smirk on the priest's face as he stood at the exit way, palm outstretched.

Back on the bus, I thought about him and what his strange smile conveyed. I recognized its meaning for myself anyway. It was a smile of contempt for those middle-aged ladies who were putting money in his hand for the privilege of being in a place where Jesus' bones were supposed to be. We had seen a dim sarcophagus. Not one of us, I think, believed we were in a hallowed spot. That outstretched hand and the contemptuous smile belied it.

I thought of those other visitors to the Holy Sepulchre in the twelfth and thirteenth centuries. That too was a fraud perpetrated on many thousands of hapless Christians by bishops and popes, knights and nobles. I refer to the ignominious Crusades called by the Church "penitential pilgrimages" to regain the Holy Sepulchre from the infidel Turks.

The abjectly poor, the genuinely pious and many criminals volunteered. They were told that their sins would be forgiven, their debts cancelled and extra merits added to shorten their stay in Purgatory. On some Crusades, three days of pillaging was permitted.

As the disorderly fanatic crowd pressed forward under knight or noble, they would burst into shouts of Hep, Hep as they neared a Jewish community. It was a deadly cry because it meant torture, rape, looting and death to the peaceful inhabitants of towns on their route, such as Orleans and Rouen in southern France.

The cry Hep is thought to be an acrostic form of the Latin words Hierosolyma est Perdita (Jerusalem is Destroyed) using the initial letters. The words are incised in the Arch of Titus in Rome, a memorial to the conqueror of Jerusalem in 70 c.e. Why wait to avenge the death of our Savior, thought the pilgrims, when we have his murderer right here. Ten thousand Jews were slaughtered in that first Crusade.

When I read about the Crusades in school, many years ago, I had been thrilled by tales of high adventure in a noble cause. Figures like Godfrey of Bouillon and Richard the Lionhearted were heroes, their cause just. Not for many years did I learn that this period presented the Church in one of its most barbarous phases.

Godfrey of Bouillon, writing to his pope after he had conquered Jerusalem and spent a week slaughtering the inhabitants, boasted how his men, their horses·wading up to their forelegs in blood, had dispatched every last Saracen.

The Jews had been herded into the synagogue and burned alive.

Another chronicler wrote:

"The Crusaders exulting, rushed to the Holy Sepulchre where Jesus was said to be buried. They raised their blood-stained hands in exultation, sobbing in an excess of joy. . . . On the morrow they put to the sword old men and young women with babes. No one was spared in the ecstasy of their religious zeal, neither man, nor woman, nor child, neither Jew nor Moslem nor Eastern Christian."

These were the gallant Crusaders of my history books. All of us attending school years ago were kept from any information that showed the Church in anything but a favorable light. As for the Jews, they did not exist. As I said elsewhere, they had been swept out of history.

Living Jews were regarded as if, somehow, they were outside of the human family and therefore expendable. Of course there were some exceptions.

"As for the Jews," Hitler told Bishop Berning in April 1933,
"I am just carrying on the same policy which the Catholic
church had adopted for 1,500 years."

The churches of Europe could have halted Hitler. He had
been sending up trial balloons to find out how far he could go.
His crematoria tells us what he found out. Christian Europe had
decided that the Jews were expendable. Some churches actively
connived at his actions; others, very few, protested.

To the powerless Jews, the Church seemed relentless and
merciless. Again with some exceptions. That any notions of a
powerful, world-dominating Jewry could ever be entertained in
the face of their helplessness suggests seriously irrational thinking. This irrationality does exist. In the Church's uneasy theology, the Jew was an imaginary demonic creature, totally
unrelated to the real ordinary Jew who lived a usual ordinary life.
The Jew who was reviled, robbed, exploited, humiliated and massacred was a product of the sick fantasy of the Church, a fantasy
which had filtered down to the masses.

In his book, *The Devil and the Jew* scholar Dr. Joshua Trachtenberg comments:

"The most vivid impression to be gained from a reading of
medieval allusions to the Jews is of a hatred so vast and
abysmal and so intense as to leave one gasping for comprehension."

The medieval mind conditioned to believe utterly in the truth
and infallibility of the religion taught by an overpowering
Church, could come to only one conclusion; Jews knew   that
Christianity was the only true faith but they perversely refused to
accept it. Such perversity could mean only one thing: The Jews
were not human. "They were the devil's own creatures, demonic
beings fighting the forces of truth and salvation with Satan's
weapons."

Church leaders did not dissuade them from this immoral
belief: many believed it themselves. Did not John/Jesus say so in
the Fourth Gospel?

Medieval Christians knew nothing of Judaism. They did not know that most of the sayings attributed to Jesus were compiled or duplicated from Jewish and rabbinic writings. They surely did not know that the Beatitudes and the Lord's prayer were reworked, well organized, Biblical, rabbinic and other Jewish texts and prayers.

To this day, the average Christian believes that the ethics and morality in his Bible are entirely original with Christianity. Some modern Jews do not know any better either. What belongs indisputably to Christianity (except some rarely used ideals) are three components: supernaturalism, vilification of Jews, and the crucifixion drama.

Jews could not understand why they were persecuted. They never looked into the Christians' Bible to find out. It represented a threat as did the very name of Jesus. The cross symbolized hatred and persecution. Some scholars might study the gospels but the average Jew kept far away. Anything to do with Christianity meant pain and sorrow. If you have ever looked at photographs of now dead Holocaust Jews, you can see the centuries of pain and sorrow in their eyes, Jewish eyes.

Jews have not understood why they were treated like defendants in some non-existent crime. They were put on perpetual trial, says author Albert Memmi, in a grotesque Kafkaesque nightmare.

One can understand how decent caring humans who absorbed the Jewish legacy of righteousness and mercy in their Christian churches could nevertheless be so indifferent to the plight of Jews over the centuries. Their understanding of Judaism itself, slight as it was, had been presented to them through a distorting mirror.

The New Testament writings, reinforced by four centuries of patristic hostility, culminated in the brilliant but bitter Church Father, St. Augustine, who brought immense power to the Church. I quote a piece of doggerel:

"St. Augustine, 'child of his mother's tears'
Brought gloom to Christians for a thousand years."

With the rise of rationalism and the revolutionary changes in industrial, economic, social and religious life, the deadly disease which is antisemitism, took forms other than the overtly religious one. But the Church had done the spade work and done it well. Its portrait of the Jew as devil, murderer of God, rapacious and conspiratorial underlay all the accusations which would be directed at him in the future.

When economic, social and political circumstances required a scapegoat, the Jew provided an acceptable victim. He could be used as a sacrifice in any struggle for power.

Because of his vaguely mysterious connection with deity in its most negative aspects, antisemitic and or cynical leaders could use the Jew as the demonic explanation for any catastrophe.

Consider the massacres and pogroms during Eastern Europe's economic and social upheavals; witness the Church's role in the Dreyfus affair in connivance with corrupt government officials. No one will forget Hitler, nor the acquiescence and support of some German churches, nor the averted eyes of Rome, fearful of Communism, nor the indifference of the rest of the western world.

There were heroic exceptions; the smallness of their number emphasized the indifference of the world.

Centuries of false indoctrination about Jews, and the ecclesiastical sanction of hatred for Jews caused the Church to pander, unwittingly perhaps, to man's "yetzer hara," his evil inclination. This is not the "original sin" of Paul and Augustine, by any means; Judaism abjures that sickly concept. The Talmudists wisely recognized the conflicting impulses in man and urged him to choose his "yetzer toba," his inclination towards good. This is the way to life. Hebrew Scriptures contain this commandment and repeat it often. The sickly joy of hating, this schaden-freude was accepted and nourished by an indifferent Church.

The writer Yuri Suhl, commenting about the sickness which is antisemitism summed it up in a tragicomic epigram: "Antisemitism," he said, "is a Christian disease fatal to Jews."

Christianity must make the decision to end antisemitism: it lies in its power to do so. The early Church hoped that Jews would accept Christianity as its truth; two thousand years have proved otherwise. Not because Jews are blind or demonic as the medieval Church insisted but because the thousand years of

Judaism which preceded Christianity, a thousand years of struggle to establish and maintain monotheism, made the death and resurrection theme unacceptable to sturdy monotheists. (Modern liberal Christians who have already demythologized this originally pagan concept, can understand.)

Outside of total genocide — something the Church has never wished or encouraged — Jews may remain the eternal people that many devout Jews believe it to be.

I remembered a television scene of the Eichmann trial, in which a man is shouting at someone in the lower arena of the court. His words echo in my mind: "You fool," he said passionately, "don't you know that we are an eternal people?"

I do not believe quite as fervently as that speaker did but I can understand how it happened that Jews are the longest-lived continuous community of people in history.

It was a different matter 2,700 years ago when the "Assyrians came down like a wolf on the fold" and captured ten tribes of Israel in north Palestine. Many fanciful legends grew up about the ten "lost" tribes. Actually they were assimilated into the Assyrian empire.

Jews have a much clearer sense of themselves than did those captured tribes of the north. Jews have been helped to this clarity and coherence by their firm and unified belief in a simple undogmatic monotheism. Since the Christian era, they have been unified by the shared experience of antisemitism, culminating in that watershed event, the Holocaust.

Because of its history with respect to Christianity, Jews may be inclined to think that the Church was chiefly occupied with the "Jewish question." This was not the case at all. The "Jewish problem" was only peripheral.

The Church had many more important matters to attend to. Their history has been a tumultuous one, ridden with dissent and dissenting sects. They had to repress "heresies," maintain orthodoxy, and work to increase their wealth, power and influence. They engaged in struggles to increase their temporal power, often fighting with or against dukes, kings and princes.

With cross and sword, they succeeded in Christianizing Europe. As author M. Dimont (*The Indestructible Jews*) puts it:

"It took ten centuries of armed conversion to establish Christianity in Europe. When the carnage was over, everyone on that continent was either Christian or dead — except the Jews."

There is a book you may want to own. It is called *Anti-Semitism: The Causes and Effects of a Prejudice,* published by Citadel Press in paperback (1979). The authors, Grosser and Halperin, dedicate the work to the victims of anti-semitism — Jews and Christians. The book surveys in brief clear paragraphs a catalogue of incidents, year by year and offers enlightening data on the background, Jewish and Christian, against which these incidents may be viewed. Scholarly and objective, it nevertheless makes absorbing reading.

Not all the crimes against Jews can be recorded in its 400 pages but those included provide a valuable reference.

On March 21, 1979, I noted an item in the New York Times about the death of a teenager, an Orthodox Jewish lad. Two young men, 22, followed him as he was escorting his young charges to their bus after attending a hockey game at Madison Square Garden. They taunted him with religious slurs. He succeeded in getting his group into their bus whereupon the youths smashed the bus window. When he got out to protest, a shoving match ensued. One of the attackers used a hammer and the teenager died soon after.

A few months later, I read in the New York Times of an attack by a gang of ten or twelve teenagers on a Jewish Seminary in Forest Hills, Queens, New York.

The youths had just been released for the summer vacation and were in high spirits. They stormed the Seminary using bats, bottles and sticks. Four seminarians were treated in the hospital; one suffered a broken nose.

When the priest of the nearby church was interviewed — apparently the boys attended a Catholic school — he deplored this evidence of antisemitism and attributed it in part to the "lack of recreational facilities in the community."

A non-Jew reading this would nod his head soberly and agree that certainly more recreational facilities were needed. A Jew reading the priest's statement would beat his breast in Biblical despair. Recreation! He would recall the accounts of his Eastern European grandparents who had been the butt of attacks and beatings as sportive peasants, released from the Easter passion services sought out the Jews for a bit of recreation — and revenge. He would recall the indignities related by pious Jews who would be mocked and tormented by hoodlums in East European villages. (In fairness, it should be said that Jews and Christians generally lived in peace when there was no provocation.)

These young students, here in the United States, were behaving like Eastern European hoodlums of an earlier period. Elated that school is out, the high-spirited boys get together for some fun. "What say, fellas," the leader suggests, "we go beat up some Yids."

I was especially sorry that a priest should be so unaware of the appalling implications of his remark that the boys beat up the Jewish Seminarians because they had no recreational outlet. Had his clerical training been limited only to learning how to perform the rites and ceremonials required?

The remark of the police precinct captain when he was interviewed by the newspaper reporter, struck me as cogent. It was a good thing, he said, that the Seminarians had not "backed off" (his words). Further violence was thus prevented from spreading.

This is perhaps a lesson for all Jews to learn. The Israelis mastered this lesson even before their State was born.

The many knotty strands of antisemitism are tightly enmeshed in the warp and woof of the Christian fabric, a blemished cloth.

The Church claims credit for civilizing the western world. My reading of history indicates that the Church represented a restraining and reactionary force. It was the individual (who happened to be a Christian) whose creative genius burst out of the Church's bonds. He brought enlightenment, scientific knowledge and humanity to the world in spite of, not because of, the Church whose record in this respect is not a glorious one.

I recall a television interview some years ago when Bernadette Devlin gave her opinion. She was the young Irish woman, an IRA fighter who had been wounded. I do not know if she is still involved in any way or whether the current IRA is the same.

At the time, my chief interest was her comment when asked how she thought the Church would react to her activism.

"Not to worry," she replied wryly. "Whichever side wins, that is the side the Church will support." I admit I was taken aback.

As for the church and civilization, it was the rise of scientific inquiry and the growing awareness of the fundamental Judaic concepts of equality and fraternity which influenced the growth of civilization, the Church notwithstanding.

When the Church chose a crucified Jew for its Lord and Savior, it adopted also his Scriptures, the Hebrew Bible. Christianity has always had available for its use, the lofty moral ideals and spiritual grandeur of the prophets and psalmists of Israel. These are in the Old Testament.

When the Church became an official religion, it defined itself by cross and sacrament. In its missionizing fervor, it had offered its converts those rites and sacraments that the religiously undeveloped proselytes could most easily understand. It did not emphasize the Judaic aspects as much.

Perhaps the reason that many converts in Africa and Latin America and other "primitive" countries are still nominal Christians may be due to the superficial nature of their understanding. In these times, we have the phenomenon of peoples who retain their pagan gods, now worshiped under the names of Christian saints.

The Christian experience is now a long one. Its thinkers and philosophers have endowed Christian doctrine with elevated meanings. The underlying Christology concept remains however. It is as alien to Jews now as it was two thousand years ago.

But the more liberal established churches, as well as individuals seem to be moving closer to the Judaic concepts of social justice. Christians always engaged in "good works" but the goal was the personal salvation of the recipient. Today, the emphasis seems to have shifted—to the greater benefit of mankind.

The anti-Judaic frenzy of those long-ago leaders of a very young, insecure sect, blown up into monstrous proportions by the interpretations of the Church Fathers no longer seems to influence space age minds. Equally important, the former victims of this frenzy will refuse any longer to be victimized in a post-Holocaust world.

VII

USURPATION AND DISTORTION

His face glowed pink-white in the clear Jerusalem sunshine as we talked that day. He had just come from a class in Judaic studies at Hebrew University.

"But it is so the same," the young Dutch seminarian exclaimed in amazement. "Everything we do and say, it is so like the Jews!" He seemed elated as well as astonished.

I understood his astonishment. I knew that Christians except for some interested scholars, had been kept in almost complete ignorance of living Judaism. The Churches preferred to ignore the existence of the vital rabbinic religion which had continued the Teaching when the Temple fell.

It still flourishes, growing and changing but maintaining its basic integrity. Jesus would find himself as comfortable in a small orthodox synagogue today, as he did two thousand years ago. He would need a scholar however to render the Hebrew into Aramaic.

The Holocaust jolted many hitherto indifferent clergymen into sudden horrified awareness; their seminary studies had not prepared them for reality. They had been soothed into comfortable complacency by the repetitious glorification of Christianity as the one and only valid religion. To be "Christian" was to be virtuous, even noble.

If a puzzled Shintoist, for example, should ask me, "Why did the Christian church keep your religion so secret, so suppressed? Christians worship Jesus who was a Jew and they use your Scriptures."

I should have to reply that the story is a long and painful one. I would say that certain beliefs fundamental to Christianity are in conflict with Jewish belief. The Church being stronger in number and power, suppressed the Jews.

Judaism continued its proselytization even after the destruction of the Temple in 70 c.e. There had been no hiatus in Jewish religious life, the rabbis at once reorganizing the worship. Prayer instead of Temple sacrifice, long used in the Diaspora was found to be an even more satisfactory substitute. The Temple was in fact and in effect obsolete. The Temple priests had never been popular and they disappeared. Despite the disparagement of church writers, Judaism was alive and in better health than before.

After the final war in 132–5, Hadrian ousted the Jews from Jerusalem and finished building a pagan shrine in place of the Temple. Although church writers had ascribed the destruction of the Temple in 70 to the failure of the Jews to recognize Jesus as messiah or Christ, no Jew saw any connection. As was usual with them, they attributed the catastrophe to their own shortcomings in not obeying the law as scrupulously as they should have.

But the slaughter and havoc wreaked by their hopeless wars against the Romans did cause a further scattering of Jews and offered the new sect an opportunity to capitalize on the misfortune, to gain more converts, many of whom had been turning to Judaism.

Christianity was now a separate religion although not officially recognized by Rome for another two hundred years. Most of the New Testament material had been written, though not yet selected, edited and canonized. Jesus had been dead for more than a century, Paul for three-fourths of a century.

It was of the most intense concern for the Christian missionizers to prove that Jesus, around whom the gospels were written, was the bona fide messiah of Hebrew Scripture. (Actually the Hebrew Bible itself had few references to a messiah; it was the later apocalyptic writing which emphasized messianic goals.)

Jews had no objection to Jesus as a messiah. There had been

messiahs before him and there would be a number after him, as we know. But the "Christ" proposed by Paul and elaborated by the evangelist John was not a Jewish messiah at all!

Paul's converts were asked to believe that an aspect of God, humanized in the form of the Jew, Jesus, undertook to be crucified in order to sacrifice himself for the sins of man (specifically for Christians who believed this idea was the truth.)

John went farther. Jesus was God's divine son. When he allowed himself to be put to death, he took on man's sins, purified their "vile bodies" so that their souls could be released and attain immortality or eternal spiritual life. (We can hear John the dualist thinker and the Gentile gnostic.)

Neither Paul's nor John's ideas were compatible with Jewish thought. Gentiles, former pagans were untroubled. Still the Church was faced with a difficult problem. Jesus was the fulcrum around which the new Christian faith revolved. With Jesus came the Hebrew Scriptures — it was part of the package, so to speak. As earnest believers in their new religion, these Gentile missionizers had to wrest the proof for Jesus' messiahship out of the Jewish Scriptures; there was no other source.

To find this proof and to make it stick, they had to accuse the Jews of not understanding the meaning of their own sacred writings. They had to discredit and damn Judaism.

To repeat, the Church had to negate Judaism in order to legitimate Christianity.

To this end, the gospels were written to include the deadly and contrived crucifixion drama. We find the unrestrained anti-Judaic outbursts in Matthew and John supposedly emanating from Jesus and the vilification of Jews throughout the gospels. These hate-filled accusations of Jews and the Jewish religion were reinforced by the writings of the Church Fathers. These latter, believing they had the one and only "truth" fought a passionately bitter war of words against the "unbelieving" Jews.

Thus the New Testament and the patristic writings in addition to centuries of polemics, homilies, treatises, sermons, testimonies, dramas, playlets, caricatures, art work and much more, provided the basis for two millennia of antisemitism which ended in the greatest planned mass killing in history.

Beginning with Paul in the first century and continuing past the Church Fathers' work in the sixth, studies show how Jewish writings had been freely used and reinterpreted to "prove" Christian contentions.

"The greatest act of robbery in history," says Dr. Bokser, "brought the Jewish Scriptures into the service of the Church. All that the great Hebrew prophets, priests and sons of the Jewish people had produced over a millennium of suffering—all their liturgy, chants and poetry, all were appropriated as if they were the rightful property of the Church which called itself the new Israel." The shocking use which the Church made of the Jewish treasure in turning on the victims of the theft has never been paralleled.

Hebrew Scripture, that majestic library of wisdom, morality and poetry which possessed also the grandeur of millennial antiquity, was used by the Church to extract meanings suitable for its own purposes whether these conformed to truth or not.

Since the new Christian sect had its origin two hundred years after the canon of Hebrew Scripture was closed, "proof" had to depend on allegorical interpretation of historical data of many centuries earlier. Eager missionaries, determined to find verification for their religious theory, turned historical fact into figurative prophecy. Everything was grist to their mill.

The Church culled enough material to include in its own Bible and named it the New Testament, indicating thereby that the Hebrew Bible was now the "Old Testament" to which the new was a sequel and a culmination.

"This perversion of the Hebrew Bible into a weapon against the Jews," says the same scholar Dr. Ben Zion Bokser, "was described by a Christian clergyman and writer, Dr. Bernhard E. Olson who comments:

"Out of their dire need, the Church Fathers argued for the originality and antiquity of Christianity . . . yet they were highly selective and invidious in their use of the Old Testament which they claimed as Church history. They claimed the prophets and heroes for the Church and reserved the villains and their villainy for the synagogue.

"Israel's failures were seen as Jewish failures but Israel's victories belonged to the Church. The Old Testament blessings and promises were appropriated for Christians while the denunciations and judgments were to fall on Jews alone.

"By means of these . . . arguments, the Jews became a theological abstraction, not a real people. The Jews were fashioned in the image of idolators, evil-doers, devils, while Christians in their own eyes became true, noble and angelic."

The learned scholar of the late nineteenth and early twentieth century, Adolph Harnack of the University of Tübingen in Germany reports these words of an early Christian writer. It is to be found in his 1904 book *Mission and Expansion of Christianity*:

"Since the Jews were deceived about the meaning of Scriptures, that is, they did not understand that it is really a preamble to Christ, they were therefore deceived in other matters, for example about being the chosen people. Actually the Christians were the chosen people, a fact which did not come to light until the arrival of Jesus Christ. The Old Testament from cover to cover has absolutely nothing to do with the Jews. Illegally and insolently, the Jews seized on it; they confiscated it; they tried to claim it as their property.

"Every Christian must therefore deny them the possession of the Old Testament. It would be a sin for a Christian to say, 'this book belongs to us and the Jews.' No, it belonged to us from the outset as it belongs forever more to none but Christians whilst Jews are the worst, the most godless and god-forsaken of all nations on earth, Satan's synagogues, a fellowship of hypocrites. They are stamped by the crucifixion of the Lord. God has now brought them to open ruin before the eyes of the world; their Temple is

burned, their city destroyed. Never again is Jerusalem to
be frequented (by them)."

A present day Jew, reading this nonsense by an early Christian, can yet recognize the intense anxiety behind those angry
words. The believer has come upon something he wishes to cling
to and he fears that the rightful owner will take it from him.

Harnack suggests that such writing was due to the Church's
instinct for self-preservation and a way of justifying their appro-
priation of Scriptures.

Harnack though considered a liberal can make no room for
Judaism. Nor for Catholicism. He can not, he says, altogether
denounce the Gentile (i.e., Catholic) Church for this attitude.
"By their rejection of Jesus," he says, "the Jewish people dealt a
deathblow to their own existence" (italics mine).

Reading this statement of his, a Jew who experiences his religion vividly must marvel at such self-satisfied assurance and complacency. The words of Amos (6:1) spring to mind: "Woe to those
who are at ease in Zion!" or the words of Emerson who said
"truth or repose; take your choice, you can't have both."

There are too many churchmen like Harnack among those
clerics and theologians who seek not truth but repose.

In sharp contrast, Dr. Rosemary Reuther's book *Faith and
Fratricide* is straightforward and unreposeful. If it is not already
so, it should be required reading in every seminary, Jewish and
Christian. Her penetrating insights, presented with no wasted
words, must be standing Christian theology on its head.

I came across a sentence of Kirssop Lake a noted church
writer of some decades ago, regretting that he found more intellectual dishonesty among theologians and clergymen than would
be tolerated in other professionals.

Theologians have been called word spinners and word game-
sters. It requires many more words to obscure truth than to
declare it. Countless millions of words have been wasted playing
the religion game and throwing up a smoke screen to cloud clear
thinking.

Jews as people are of course recognized as having an existence but Judaism as a religion is still not recognized as such by

the ultra orthodox Catholic church. We need only recall the words of the late Cardinal Bea who declared that with the advent of Jesus Christ, Judaism no longer had a function.

Underlying this plainly false statement as millions of Jews will testify, may lurk the unexpressed fear among theologians that an acceptance of Judaism's existence predicates a denial of Christianity's legitimacy.

As we said earlier, church writers sought verification for what they already believed to be true. The only source was Scripture. This they studied laboriously, word by word, sentence by sentence. Where any phrase or line admitted of an interpretation they could use, they seized on it. That vast cornucopia which is the Septuagint (the Hebrew Bible in Greek) was examined tirelessly and minutely to make it yield up evidence to lend credence to the role they believed was Jesus'.

The famous "suffering servant" passage (Isaiah 53:3–5) was one of their greatest finds, as they pursued their digging into this thousand-year-old mine. They considered it positive proof that Jesus' "the man of sorrows" had been foretold. It fitted perfectly.

But the "suffering servant" was undoubtedly a metonym for the people Israel as modern scholars agree. One scholar thought Isaiah may even have been referring to himself. Isaiah wrote the verse about five hundred years before the Christian era and was writing of his own time.

The early Christians however seized on the text as applicable to Jesus. Modern Christian scholars acknowledge that this interpretation, so important at that time, was wishful thinking. Isaiah's words, they say, could apply to almost any martyr; they give Gandhi as an example.

An anecdote is related about a clergyman of the nineteenth century who sued the publisher of Graetz's work. Heinrich Graetz (1817–1891) the learned Jewish historian had correctly explained the famous "suffering servant" passage in Isaiah. The irate cleric accused Graetz of falsifying if not actually desecrating Christian belief!

A second-century church writer Irenaeus is often quoted for his statement, "If the Jews knew to what use we would put their

Scriptures, they would not have hesitated to burn them all."
Irenaeus was of course ignorant of the fact that Jews would never
destroy a single letter of their sacred writings. Old, disused material that might contain the name of God, was buried or stored.
(The Genizah (storehouse) in the old Ezra synagogue in Cairo
yielded up thousands of fragments from the Middle Ages when it
was discovered late in the 19th century. The Dead Sea Scrolls of
Qumran discovered in 1947 dating from before the common era
are another example.)

Justin Martyr, another second-century writer, an apologist for
Christian belief, falsifies a statement by the Latin historian,
Tacitus. The latter, reporting on the crucifixion says that Jesus
was put to death by Pontius Pilate. Justin substitutes the word
under. Thus his statement reads: Jesus was crucified under
Pilate, instead of Tacitus' comment that Jesus was crucified by
Pilate. This quiet substitution of sub for per remains part of
Christian interpretation. This wording appears even today in the
Apostles' Creed.

For good measure, the anti-Judaic Justin in his *Dialogue with
Trypho* continues "Jesus was crucified under Pilate, by your
people, Trypho." Trypho is the fictional Jew of the *Dialogue*.

Nietzsche, that brilliant sick hater of both Christianity and
Judaism, in his book *Morgenröte* (Dawn) Aphorism 84, comments
about Christian usurpation:

> "What can one expect of a religion which in the centuries
> of its foundation performed this unheard of philological
> feat in regard to the Old Testament. I mean the attempt
> to withdraw the Old Testament from the Jews asserting
> that it contained nothing but Christian doctrine and
> belongs in truth to the Christians, true people of Israel
> whereas the Jews had merely abrogated its possession to
> themselves. The Christians gave themselves up to a pas-
> sion for reinterpretation and substitution, a process which
> could not possibly have been compatible with a good con-
> science. However much the Jewish scholars protested, it
> was affirmed that everywhere in the Old Testament, the
> theme was Christ and only Christ."

The Catholic missionary magazine *The Bridge* in a 1961 volume quotes a poem by one Cardinal Stefanescki in which he includes the phrase that the Torah is "pregnant with Christ." (Reported by Dr. Bokser in his book *Judaism and the Christian Predicament.*)

Orthodox Catholic and Protestant churchmen, particularly the excessively missionary-minded, not only insist that Christianity is the fulfillment of Judaism but they insist on trying to get Jews to believe this. To this end, they quote and cite the misreadings, the mistranslations, the distortions and the falsifications of the early Christian apologists. These modern missionaries do not think of questioning their sources. "Faith and habit" have reinforced and indurated their belief. The result is the indoctrinated and conditioned theologian or cleric.

Luckily, individual Christians do not seem to get such a heavy dose of indoctrination. They seem willing to live and let live. Unlike professional religionists. Driving through Big Spring, Texas some years ago, I saw a huge billboard on Main Street (Route 80) which read, THEY THAT WAIT ON THE LORD (JESUS) WILL BE SAVED. ISAIAH.

Had I stopped to talk to the preacher of the local church which had put up the sign, he no doubt would have told me in some surprise that of course Isaiah meant Jesus when he wrote those words. Isaiah was a prophet; the whole of the Hebrew Bible, he would tell me, is simply a prophecy about Jesus. Didn't I know that? That was Christian truth!

We Jews are an ancient people. We have learned patience and tolerance. We have had to live (and die) with Christian "truth." We know however that in time when Christianity is at peace with herself theologically she will not try to destroy Jewish truth and Jews with it. And the Church will cease its attempts to missionize the Jews.

For missionizing is a more subtle expression of that fear and hostility which during the Middle Ages took the form of outright persecution.

After the age of reason and the Emancipation, the fear and hostility were expressed in other quasi-sociological forms, until it broke out in its most demonic and murderous form in the Holocaust.

The peg, the handle, the hook from which attacks on Jews depended, was the deicide charge. Jews had killed God. Was anything, could anything be more heinous, more deserving of the strongest possible punishment?

We can not go into the dynamics of the unconscious and irrational fears which allowed the primitive image of the Jew to persist over the centuries. Suffice to say that it did. It was rationalized around a single theme which the church writers, beginning with the gospels used over and over again. The Jews, said these writers, have <u>always slain their prophets,</u> the last of whom — and this was <u>their climactic denouement</u> — was Jesus, savior, messiah, god.

The crucifixion story used this theme and the evangelist John, placed the blame for Jesus' death entirely on the Jews in his gospel. Slaying the prophets became a popular slogan; it paved the way to the deicide slogan which led ultimately to Auschwitz.

This slogan was based on just two stories in all the vast literature of the Hebrew Bible: In the tenth century B.C.E. (1 Kings 19:10) the prophet Elijah, that doughty champion of God's law is complaining to God that idolatrous Jews had forsaken the covenant, thrown down their altars and slain their prophets. Now they were after him too.

His story begins some verses earlier. Elijah had thundered against the wicked Jezebel who has persuaded her husband Ahab to follow her sinful and idolatrous ways. She has slain many prophets of God. In retaliation, Elijah slew many prophets of Baal. Now they are after him. This is the first instance of Jews slaying their prophets.

The second mention of prophet slaying occurs in the fifth century B.C.E. (Nehemiah 9:26). Here the prophet complains about the disobedient people of the time who "rebelled, cast the law behind their backs, slew the prophets who urged them to turn back to God, and who wrought great provocation." But four verses later, Nehemiah addresses God, "nevertheless thou didst not forsake them for thou art a gracious and merciful God."

There is mention of a ninth century B.C.E. Zechariah (not the prophet), upon whom the spirit of God came and he reproached the people for their transgressions (2 Chronicles 24:20). King Joash ordered him stoned. But this tale is in a different category.

That is the lot! Two instances of prophet-slaying in a thousand-year history! On this paltry evidence — which was anyway an in-house matter for the ancient Jews — a huge juggernaut of vilification, calumny and appalling persecution was constructed to crush an innocent people.

The aim of the church writers was to convince generations of Christians that Jews were accursed and deicidal. Had they not slain (as was their habit) the last and greatest prophet, Jesus, son of God?

The eloquent St. John of Antioch (Chrysostom) coined the word "deicide" which was translated into every language of every country already Christian, and those to be converted to Christianity. "Christ-killer" was a familiar epithet used to attack and torment small Jewish boys who did not understand what it meant but suffered deep anguish. It is rarely heard in our country now but I remember it well.

Further probing into Hebrew Scriptures by diligent exegetes helped unearth enough suggestions, clues, pointers and hints that could be useful, with some bending of meaning, to serve the Christian purpose. They found evidence of resurrection proof in Ezekiel's "dry bones which had been clothed with flesh and given breath" (Ezekiel 37:7 ff). They found in Daniel the clue that "many that sleep shall awake" (Daniel 12:2).

There was no dearth of material. The researchers struck gold of another kind in the Prophets. When these mighty voices called God's people to account for their transgressions, for defeat in some military enterprise as due to deviating from God's commandments, for some catastrophe for failing to hew to God's word, the Church writers seized on each word. When Isaiah upbraided the Jews because they were invaded by Persia; when Jeremiah castigated them for not behaving like the holy ones of God; when Micah excoriated the rulers of Jacob for their transgressions, Church researchers gathered up every word of reproach to use in their own diatribes against the Jews. Here from their own prophets were accusations affirming that Jews were a sinful, apostate people!

When, however, the prophets having hurled their thunder-bolts, now offered their people the glories and joys which were to come as the repentant, the beloved of God, all these promises and joys were diverted by Church writers as applying to Christians. All the howlings, threats and curses were aimed at Israel; all the bliss and promises of glory belonged to Christians.

On a table, I have an outsized King James Bible dated 1883. It opens easily to Isaiah and I read the editor's notations. On top of the page which shows the date (712 before Christ), I see such chapter headings as: "The blessings of Christ's kingdom"; "The privileges of the Gospel"; "God's love for the Church"; or "The glorious access of the Gentiles into the Church" and much more. On the other hand, I note "the Jews' hypocrisy," "the Jews' dereliction," "the idolatry of the Jews," and much more.

I looked again and yes, this is the Jewish Scriptures. I see that the entire Hebrew Bible has been annotated to show that, on the one hand, the Jews (whose Book this is) are apostate, idolators, derelict sinners and hypocrites. On the other hand, Christ is foretold as coming to bring joy to all in his blessed kingdom. And the busy Church researchers cite chapter and verse in proof!

Since nothing in the Hebrew Bible can possibly have any connection with the activities of Jesus, called Christ, since he was born some two centuries after the Bible was canonized and ten or twelve centuries in some instances before the "proofs," Jews can only marvel. Was it "pious fraud?" Was it extreme naiveté? It could have been either or both.

The current Bibles are quite different, fortunately, than the one I cited. In 1952, the revised edition of the King James Bible made notable changes. The 1964 Confraternity edition (under Catholic auspices) has excluded editorial tampering. The Anchor Bible and the Interpreter's Bible are works of modern and combined scholarship.

Although progress continues and here we must be grateful to continuing Biblical scholarship, the core of the problem exists. Masses of people still continue to read edited Bibles. Simple believers who have no reason to think that the "Good Book" would lie, can lean back comfortably, assured by the knowledge that Christians are the blessed people and that the ancient Jews are cursed.

Masses of people have only a superficial knowledge of either religion. Troubled people look for fixed, positive certainties in an uncertain world. They prefer not to ask questions which may unsettle them. They are afraid.

The hard nut of Jewish-Christian relations remains. Dr. Reuther puts a nerve-wracking question to orthodox Christian theology: "Is it possible," she asks, "to eliminate anti-Judaism and still affirm Jesus as Christ?"

The question will be pondered by ecclesiastics and probably ignored or evaded by Christians in general. For the latter, if they are not suffering from antisemitic bias, the question is of no serious personal concern. To Jews who are vulnerable, the question will be fraught with feeling, especially if they are uninformed Jews. They do not know that they have been victims of a gigantic fraud whose perpetrators have themselves been deceived.

Volumes could be filled in recording the infamous language used to defame the Jew. The purpose of those early "interpreters" was a fixed and determined need to demonstrate the inferiority of Judaism and Jews and to contrast their baseness with the spiritual fulfillment to be found in Christianity.

Deliberate mistranslations of psalms to wrest meanings favorable to Christians and debasing to Jews was one method. Twisting parables so they would favor the Christian point of view was another.

At the same time, Christian liturgy, celebrations, services all called upon the magnificent grandeur of Prophets and Psalms to glorify and aggrandize their own rituals. Hebrew chants became the Gregorian chants; Hebrew poetry and prayer became the liturgical base for their ceremonies. As that Dutch seminarian said in wonder, "Everything we do, it is so like the Jews."

Jews did not expect thanks for the use of their heritage. They did not expect gratitude. Some Jews believed it was God's plan that monotheism and Jewish ethics be disseminated over the world. Jews have not understood however why they were nearly annihilated instead. It is not easy to understand irrationality.

One of the most famous and irrational haters of Jews was the previously mentioned Chrysostom. This ascetic reformer seems to become rabid in his denunciations of Jews and their synagogues.

Most noteworthy is his intense preoccupation with the flesh. His "golden mouth" hissed poisonous venom whenever he spoke of the "lustful" Jews in their "brothel" synagogues.

From an 1888 translation of a Greek book called *Leaves of St. John Chrysostom,* I glanced at his case history. John was born in the year 347, the only son of a rich woman who became widowed early in life. She refused to remarry, preferring to devote her life and love to him.

Baptized at age 22, he became a bishop at age 26. Feeling unworthy, he fled home to live among anchorites in the mountains near Antioch. There he spent four years in a cavern practicing austerities of such severity that his health failed and he returned to Antioch. Here he preached for ten years and gained his reputation for eloquence. He wrote 486 homilies on the New Testament, more than half of these on Paul. His eight scurrilous sermons on Jews and Judaizers should perhaps be placed in the "rare books" department of a library with access only for mature readers who can understand his sickness and not be influenced by his sorry words.

A trained Freudian might suggest that, like St. Augustine, his problems may have arisen out of the possibly unwholesome attachment to him of his mother Anthusa. (Her name has also been given as Drusilla.)

The author of the term "deicide" must have found the optimistic attitude of Jews towards life's joys, a hateful reminder of his own suppressed needs. He would find in attacking Jews an acceptable "Christian" outlet for his anger and guilt. We remember that he was primarily railing against fellow-Christians who found Judaism attractive and who continued to share their feasts and services (Jews had been inhabitants of Antioch for 600 years and were at ease there).

Perhaps Chrysostom may himself have felt the allure of contact with normal, non-self-punishing people. By castigating the Jews and their Judaizer friends, he was probably administering punishment to himself. We may certainly speculate that this was so.

His contemporaries, the Church Fathers St. Jerome and St. Augustine, also had an unhealthy attitude about sex. Like

Chrysostom (an admirer of the like-minded Paul), those two Church Fathers found the flesh filthy and sinful. St. Jerome especially, while he had a prurient interest in sex, seemed especially to find squalor and an unkempt appearance in his women servants a requisite.

St. Gregory of Nyssa, another contemporary, called Jews the

"murderers of the lord, assassins of the prophets, rebels, detesters of God, calumniators, companions of the devil, race of vipers, informers, darkeners of the mind, enemies of all that is beautiful. . . ."

We read these hysterical ravings of frustrated ascetics (all sainted) and we recognize the sickness of soul that prompted their words. But the effect of these words as they filtered down to the ignorant masses may be seen in the appalling history of the Church as it attacked the unsuspecting Jews.

I found the "Confessions" of St. Augustine illuminating in understanding his avoidance of sex. He tells us of his mother Monica—she too was sainted—and her "too earthly love for me." He reports how passionately she clung to him when he had to board the boat to Rome.

Although he had a son by a concubine in his early youth, he returned to ascetic ways in his search for happiness. He concluded that only in the "city of God" could one find it. Apparently, he had to flee his mother's (and perhaps his own) strong attachment, by living a celibate life.

"A brilliant man and a subtle theologian," says Dr. Muller, "he was also a deeply unhappy one. Millions of Christians were victims of his frustrations since his writings strongly influenced Christian doctrine."

While he taught his pupils that Jews had tortured and killed Christ, his invective is less rabid. Indirectly however he inflicted frightful harm on Jews who also became victims of his dogma. The ignorant believers, anticipating the tortures of hellfire and damnation with which he threatened Christendom, relieved their anxiety by persecuting Jews, embodiment of the very devil they would find in hell.

It was this theological Jew which the Christians knew.

"This grotesque caricature drawn by the church fathers was not a human being at all," says Dr. Parkes. "He is a theological abstraction, a monster of superhuman cunning and malice. . . he is drawn from the perspective of a distorting mirror."

VIII

THE GREAT BRAINWASH

Millie was telling me that Charlene Wright, a teaching colleague for many years, had just died. "She was a true Christian," Millie said in final eulogy.

I restrained my irritation; Millie is a Jew with little knowledge either of Judaism or Christianity.

"How do you define a true Christian?" I asked cautiously.

She was taken aback. "Well, uh, you know. She was a kind, considerate woman. Sort of spiritual."

"Would you call Dorothy a true Christian?" She is a mutual friend.

Millie stared at me in astonishment. "Dorothy is Jewish; you know that."

"But she is kind, considerate and very spiritual."

Millie made a gesture of annoyance. I took another tack. "Remember all that 19th-century literature we read in college?"

"Mmm," Millie nodded.

"Do you remember those phrases: "He was a true Christian gentleman" or "She practiced true Christian love" or "That was not very Christian of you."

"I certainly do," Millie was beginning to grasp my meaning.

"And in high school," I went on, "for required reading we had

131

the Jew Shylock and the Jew Fagin. Remember?"

"That was half a century ago," Millie reminded me. "Another world."

"True," I said. But I knew it was only partly true.

A television picture flashes into my mind in clear color. A Central American general in a creased uniform is mouthing words. "We are a Christian nation," he is saying. Behind him lie the slain corpses of his fellow countrymen. The general repeats his words and asks for more military aid.

What does it mean, being a Christian? Does it mean baptism and the eucharist? Or more sacraments if a Catholic. Or does it mean not hating your brother in your heart, not doing to others what is hateful to you, loving your neighbor as yourself, caring for the needy and being merciful and compassionate.

If it means the latter, then you have learned the Jewish virtues. Not all Jews practice all of them but if as a Christian you do practice them you may be called a true Jew.

Gotthold Ephraim Lessing, a Christian writer, critic, liberal thinker and dramatist wrote a play called *Nathan the Wise*. He had his close friend, Moses Mendelssohn in mind when he wrote it. Mendelssohn, philosopher and writer, initiated the Jewish "enlightenment" in the eighteenth century.

In the play, the following dialogue occurs. Responding to the Lay Brother who says to Nathan, "By heaven, you are a Christian; there never was a better Christian," Nathan replies, "What makes me a Christian to you, makes you a Jew to me."

Both have the same qualities whether learned from the original sources in the Jewish Scriptures and rabbinic writings or from the gospel sayings attributed to Jesus.

Jews have had no reservation about Christian adoption of their Bible. The manner in which it was adapted however and the deadly use against Jews to which the New Testament was put, has mocked every noble precept of the Hebrew Bible.

From a 1933 book written by Conrad Moehlman, Professor of Christianity at Colgate-Rochester Divinity School, I quote this passage which he cites:

"We have taken your Bible and made it ours with never a

word of appreciation for the genius of God which produced it. Through all the Christian centuries, our ritual has rested on yours. We have called peace a Christian attitude forgetting that it was a Jew who first used the words that now belong to humanity about beating our swords into plowshares, and our spears into pruning hooks."

There are some Jewish thinkers who believe that Christianity's adoption of our sacred writings is part of God's divine plan. One such is Franz Rosenzweig who originated the idea that Christianity's role is that of carrier of the truth of Judaism to all the world so all mankind can reach the Father. Jews who have already reached the Father must, as a people of priests, hallow the name of God through holiness. Christians who can reach the Father only through Christ have their work still ahead, that is, to bring the message of Judaism to the Gentiles. When this is done, Christ will no longer be their Lord and the Jews no longer be the chosen. The eternal day will have arrived.

Following his thought, it is clear that Christianity can have no mission to the Jews; its work lies elsewhere until that day which signals the coming of God's messianic kingdom.

A number of outstanding theologians have been influenced by Rosenzweig's thinking but most older European and conservative Protestants and Catholics do not agree; they find they can not give up their deeply indoctrinated belief that the one and continuing way to God is through Christ. Some of them find the "intractability" of the Jews a cause of anger with its dangerous obverse — anti-Judaic feeling.

This anti-Judaism is seen by some deeply wounded and scarred Jews as possible precursors to another Auschwitz.

I am led to reflect on the Church's insistence that theirs is a religion of love, offering as proof the voluntary self-sacrifice of Jesus on behalf of (Paul's) sinful man. In contrast the God of the Jews has been presented as stern and vengeful.

But the God that the Jews worshipped then and now was Jesus' Father in heaven, the very same God. He was that merciful gracious and compassionate God found in the Hebrew Bible, which was also Jesus' Bible.

The Church writers in their zeal to damn the Jews forgot that. Or did they?

Every teacher knows how effective are the techniques of simplification and repetition. Repetition and more repetition serve to condition thinking and behavior. The centuries-long lies about the stubborn, unregenerate, accursed, deicidal Jew, hated by God, were transmitted in Church and related teachings to generation after generation of susceptible young minds. Countless millions of innocent children were conditioned to scorn and hate; their innocent Jewish counterparts reacted with fear and a sense of unworthiness. Both were "brainwashed."

Brainwashing, so-called, means the subtle insinuation and substitution of one set or system of thoughts and beliefs in place of another. In this sense my use of the word "brainwash" is not correct. I use this term even though it is not exactly accurate but because it has the pejorative and negative connotation I want to convey.

As I think about innocent children and the damage inflicted on them, I recall an episode. This may not be the place for it but then, there is really no place for it anywhere.

In 1944, truckloads of Hungarian men, women and children were brought to Auschwitz. Hitler saw that the war was going against him and that the liberating armies might come too soon for him to complete his mission.

In a fever of frenzy, he gathered up all the Jews he could and kept the death factories working night and day. It was a heavy schedule for the crematoria; they were filled to bursting. To accelerate the killing, a huge bonfire was built. (Bonfire originally meant a fire for burning bones or corpses.) Piles of wood and petrol were heaped up.

Nazi guards seized the children and tossed them into the flames. To drown their screams, a band of inmates was ordered to play as loud as possible, waltz tunes from Rosamunde or The Blue Danube. In the waiting transports, two kilometers away, the others could hear the shrieks of the children being burned alive.

A guard might occasionally batter the skull of a baby before tossing it on the fire. But there was not enough time for such acts of mercy; other children were waiting their turn in nearby trucks.

Several thousand babies and young children were thus disposed of. Their parents would later be gassed and cremated. In the Holocaust more than a million children were murdered.

After I read this eyewitness report, I turned to other related reading. I noted that some theologians were having a general discussion about the concentration camps. With learned objectivity, they brought up such questions as to whether the Jews in the death camps were redeemed; whether they remained unregenerated; whether the cross retains its redemptive power.

I visualize them, these thinkers, leaning back reflectively in their comfortable leather armchairs, sipping a cognac or perhaps some sherry as they ponder these theologic profundities.

In another context, one theologian—could it have been Tillich?—remarked in an exaltation of feeling, "When I think of the suffering, the sublimity of the suffering in the camps. . . ."

Or Jacques Maritain, a noted French theologian who said, "I see the passion (suffering) of the Jews in the camps more and more taking the shape of the cross." Elsewhere he wrote how he regretted that Jews had "chosen the world." He meant presumably that they were more concerned with the problems of man on earth than in preparing for the world beyond.

Although he has been cited as a friend of Jews—his wife and collaborator was a converted Jew—I would guess that Maritain was and remained a theological (and emotional) antisemite.

Every literate person of my generation knew Edward Gibbon's *The Decline and Fall of the Roman Empire.* A rationalist, skeptic and admirer of Voltaire, he had shocked Christendom by attributing the fall of the Roman Empire to the growth of Christianity. He further upset the Christian world by his statement that relatively few Christians had died as martyrs of Roman persecution.

(Early Christians had a passion for martyrdom, we are told. A comment by the Roman pro-consul Antoninus Pius of the second century is reported: "Are there not enough cliffs, precipices, ropes that they (the Christian ecstatics) must seek to provoke arrest and death?")

Gibbon's work which was attacked and praised for more than a century, though it deals with Christianity, seem to be oblivious of Judaism. Where he does mention it, he derogates it attributing Christianity's faults to its derivation from Judaism. Since for him, Judaism had ceased to exist, he could find only in Islam an example of true monotheism.

We should not have been surprised therefore that Toynbee, 160 years later, described Judaism as a "fossil" religion. Christians had been "brainwashed" into this belief.

Negation of the Jews was fostered and developed over the centuries by a conditioning of Christian minds to believe that Jews were despicable and contemptible. Of what value is the opinion of an unbeliever if he is a worthless non-person?

Accusations against the Jews, drawn up in the writings of the Church Fathers and others, were of course totally false and without foundation. The portrait of the Jews, a product of frustration, rivalry and fear, was based not on any reality but on the demonized image of the "theologic" Jew.

Christians subjected to these falsities may be described as being "brainwashed" into a set of beliefs, incompatible with truth.

We witnessed the results of fifteen hundred years of false indoctrination in its final stage the ethical nihilism of the Holocaust.

During the one hundred and fifty or more years between the "emancipation" and Hitler, Jews were spared outright massacre except in the sporadic pogroms in Eastern Europe. Jews had been granted civil rights following the French Revolution at varying times in different countries under different rulers and with varying conditions attached.

The punishment felt most painfully by "emancipated" Jews was the refined torture of ostracism and denial of full creative expression. We know how that long imprisoned spirit took wing, how the air of freedom catalyzed the creative spark, and how suppressed talents exploded when pressure was removed. Learning had always been a way of life to Jews to whom learning and religion were one. But the new secular knowledge outside the Torah exhilarated the new generation of Jews.

Jews' achievements were disproportionate to their numbers and they stood out, more precisely because they were Jews. But they were not allowed to enjoy their freedom fully; restraints were placed on them. Many Jews, especially in Germany, had to accept baptism in order to gain some entry into the dominant culture. Many suffered acutely; some committed suicide. Again the punishing hand of the Church lay on them, not with sword or fire on their body but on their minds and hearts.

I think of the many Jews of my generation who suffered agony and frustration because of the subtle bullying, the hostility, the discrimination they experienced as sensitive, often painfully sensitive young people. I think of how the sense of their own worth was impaired; I think of their efforts to submerge their Jewish identity in order to "belong" and of their inevitable failure, whether in fact or in their own eyes.

I can understand how many Jews turned to "causes" which held out the hope that they could merge their own rejected identity with an ideal where all mankind would be brethren.

I can also understand the circumstances that propelled so many Jews to seek, as an outlet for their private grief, the role of comedians and humorists. And where they used, as they often did on stage, the "ethnic" humor of minorities; it takes no great insight to understand this device of self-deprecation. Turning on oneself first takes the initiative away from the adversary, "softens him up" and leaves him weaponless.

Even in this country at this time in its history, there still linger restraints for Jews. They are still absent from the really top executive positions in certain banking, automotive and other corporate enterprises. In spite of the myth about moneyed Jews, the important money is in the hands of Episcopalians and Presbyterians. Jews have achieved middle-class status, lower, middle and some upper. But they are very scarce at the top. They have been prominent in the arts and sciences, in business, entertainment and scholarship. They have been serving in government with distinction and may someday aspire to the Presidency.

When Jews finally present themselves openly and comfortably as Jews, when they stop being concerned about keeping a "low profile," the idea of "Jew" may lose some of its emotional content. Christians can be reconditioned out of their "brainwashed" past. Familiarity does away with that alienating sense of difference which has been imposed on the dominant majority.

Jews also need to be reconditioned out of their "brain-washed" past. The young generation of Jews shows how simple it really is. I see them as poised and self-confident, at ease for the most part in a world which is theirs. They are unaware of the humiliations which their grandparents experienced. They engage in athletics, they are taller and straighter; their expectations are greater and for good reasons. They attend colleges which are mostly free of quotas. They have access to professions and most enterprises. They have social freedom and they take advantage of it.

I think of my own generation in the persons of two men whose award ceremonies I watched on television. The one who had been granted a high award for his many years of meritorious service as a Hollywood producer was overcome with emotion as he accepted his trophy. In his brief speech, he could only think to say that if he could be reborn, he would want to be born again as a WASP. Here he mentioned the white Anglo-Saxon Protestant director who was his reincarnation ideal.

The other man, also overcome with emotion as he received his award for his long productive career, called out to a younger associate, a celebrity and a WASP. The camera showed the puzzled (and annoyed) look on the face of this handsome and poised man as he went to the platform. I think he did not understand that the award recipient needed his support.

I watched these little dramas on the television screen with a good deal of regret. I regretted that these two useful and worthwhile men had been so beaten down psychically that they needed the emotional support they could get from the "ins," the assured WASPS. I told myself that these men were sons of poor immigrants, that they must have been taunted as "Christ-killers" in their childhood and that they had had to endure the social sneers of their time. That was why they comported themselves as they did. But an explanation only explains; it does not alter the past.

Summer time is rerun time on television. I was watching Ed Bradley a member of the "Sixty Minutes" team as he interviewed the French Rothschild at his estate in France. The Baron was eighty years old at the time still active with his vineyards and still, as he said archly, interested in women.

When at the end of the segment, Bradley asked him whether

he considered himself French or Jewish, the Baron was genuinely horrified. "French of course," he exclaimed, "one hundred percent!"

"And Jewish?" the interviewer persisted. With a half-smile and a mocking gesture, Rothschild indicated the proportion with his hand: "Five percent, maybe," he replied.

I wondered what he thought of the newspaper report on casualties when the synagogue in Rue Copernic in Paris was bombed. The journalist had made a separate tally of the number of French and the number of Jews who were hurt!

I was interested in reading about one of the 19th-century Rothschilds, Baron Lionel, the first Jewish member of the British Parliament in whose behalf the part of the Oath which includes "on the faith of a Christian" was omitted, permitting him in 1858 to take the seat to which he had been elected a number of times.

Phil Donahue of the "Donahue" show seemed to be having a little difficulty this morning. Ordinarily this best of talk show hosts glides effortlessly, it seems, through the often-difficult hour-long event. Today his guests were young couples married or about to be married, of whom the non-Jewish partner was planning to convert to Judaism.

Seated on stage in a "laid back" fashion was a prominent rabbi. He viewed the proceedings with what I thought was a complacent eye and interrupted with what I thought were unnecessary comments.

First I must mention the Christian lady who asked with a perfectly straight face whether it was true that ". . . synagogues gave their members money to start a business for three times."

A simple surprised "no" from one or two of the speakers on the dais presumably answered her question. Every Jew, I think, must have recognized the hostility in her query, her real question being "what are otherwise fine young Christians doing, converting to Judaism?"

Donahue addressed one of the couples about their decision. The young woman, a slim, shy girl said, "I'm the Jewish partner." From the platform, the rabbi called out, "You look Jewish." From the girl came a faltering voice and the plaintive words: "And all my life I have been told I do not look Jewish."

Donahue handled that one with his usual skill but I felt my skin prickle and my face get hot with compassion for the girl and annoyance with the rabbi. Probably he had meant nothing by his comment; to him the girl looked Jewish and apparently he felt obliged to say so. Why? What troubled me most was her defensive counter to the "charge" that she looked Jewish. She saw "looking Jewish" as a disparagement apparently. I doubt the rabbi had anything disparaging in mind. I think he just wanted to participate in the proceedings.

If that girl had only felt honestly able to say, "Thank you, rabbi. I'm glad you think I look like my noble ancestors, like maybe Esther the queen." But no, we are still brainwashed; our models of beauty are still stereotypical.

Many many years ago, when I was in the third or fourth grade, three of us were walking home from school to our slum neighborhoods of mixed nationalities. Estelle Band was a different kind of Jewish child; both her mother and grandmother had been born here. Our other companion was a child with an Irish name, poorly dressed, unkempt and unwashed. The reason I recall this long ago incident was because Estelle leaned over to the Irish child, "I don't look Jewish, do I?" she pleaded. I think it was the pleading in her voice that kept this memory clear to me.

This was probably the first time the little girl had been asked her opinion about anything. Until then she may not have known that "looking Jewish" was bad and that she had the power to make a decision about it.

The writer Albert Memmi in his *Liberation of the Jew* made a pointed comment. "Jews," he said, "have been accomplices in their own misery."

Even at age eight or nine, Estelle Band fitted this description.

In other matters as well, the author Memmi offers some valuable insights into the dilemma of the Jew. Because the Jew has been put on trial for so long as if he were a defendant, he acts like one. As long as he submits to this role for which he has been conditioned over centuries, he will have to defend himself.

I believe that the Jew will have to take the initiative. He must change his role from that of defendant to that of claimant. As he frees himself of the hold which this "brainwashing" has had on him, he will also free the Christian from his own thralldom.

But the Jew needs to know the source of the charges in order to refute them. He will soon learn they are only invented, without any basis in fact. They are stubbornly held, cherished because of their great age, believed because they have not been contradicted and defended because there are advantages to be gained from perpetuating the falsehoods.

When the Jew was in a state of enslavement, without any power or rights, he could only retreat and try to survive. Now he feels stronger. The time to push for improvement and change is when the yoke is lightest. His weapons need not be force. As always they will be knowledge and conviction of his truth. His own heritage must become his possession. And when as a Jew he understands Christianity, he will find himself more, much more at home with Judaism.

IX

CAN THE CHURCH LET GO?

Perhaps you know the story of the original Siamese twins, Chang and Eng. Of Chinese descent, they were born in Siam (Thailand) in 1811. Their bodies were inextricably joined at birth.

A Nantucket sea captain brought them as youths to the United States and exhibited them for some years in circuses here and abroad.

When they rebelled against their life in freak shows, they left, settled in North Carolina, married two sisters and raised large families.

Their joined bodies became in time, a frightful burden to them. Chang's habits and disposition distressed his brother gravely. Then in 1874, Chang fell ill and died. His brother Eng, though healthy died two hours later, doctors said of terror.

This story is a metaphor of sorts for the Jewish-Christian relationship. The two religions are distinct entities, inseparably joined and they are a serious burden to one another. With a difference. For it appears to be Christianity which insists on the tie. Judaism wishes to be a single autonomous entity but the Church will not let go. Individual Christians are for the most part quite indifferent except for some of the missionary-minded and those who have been contaminated with the virus of antisemitism.

Some years ago I drove to Middletown, New York to attend a Holocaust memorial. A friend, a resident there, had urged me to come.

The high school auditorium was almost full. Middle-aged and elderly couples, all neatly dressed, made up most of the audience. There were some younger couples and a scattering of youthful individuals.

What, I wondered, were so many non-Jews doing there. Perhaps it was the mild April weather and interest in a local event. They surely had had no personal experience of the Holocaust. More likely, they admired the speaker, a hard-working teaching nun, known for her efforts in behalf of Jewish-Christian amity.

Earlier I had observed a young woman directly across the aisle from me. Her companion, probably her husband, was holding her tightly clenched hand in both of his.

The speaker was late and harried-looking. First she asked for a minute of silence in memory of the two million Armenians who had been massacred, over two decades, early in the twentieth century by order of the Turkish ruler who wished to rid his country of them.

Many in the audience looked puzzled but dutifully bowed its collective head. I assumed the speaker meant to indicate a connection between that slaughter and the Holocaust even though the genocide of the Armenians was a national-political act and the Holocaust resulted from nineteen centuries of Christian anti-Judaism.

At first, the speaker placed responsibility for the Holocaust on the action of a madman, Hitler. Then apparently facing up to her subject, she spoke of the reality of Christian antisemitism. She explained that the gospels and the patristic writings needed to be understood in the context of the time and the circumstances when they were produced.

She said that the Catholic church which she represented was trying to educate students in their schools to a better understanding of Christian belief and thus minimize the anti-Judaic prejudice which has in the past been a concomitant of New Testament teaching.

Many questions were asked of her, chiefly by Jews. She did the best she could but none were satisfactorily answered. No really satisfying answer could ever be given, I thought.

The meeting was over. As my friend and I rose to leave, I noticed that the girl across the aisle was crying. In a tearful voice, she said to her companion, "They'll never let go of us, never, never!" Walking behind, we heard her despair as she asked, "Why can't they let us go?"

My friend told me later that the young woman's parents were death camp survivors. The families of both her parents had been murdered, all of them.

During the drive back to Manhattan, I kept hearing, "They'll never let go of us." A news item of the day before came to mind. Another synagogue had been vandalized; swastikas and hate words had been smeared on the walls.

The survey I mentioned elsewhere which gave the percentage of antisemites as being thirty-five percent, noted also that clergymen on the whole tended to be more antisemitic than their non-clerical, professional counterparts.

My thoughts returned to that girl in Middletown. Perhaps the sight of her parents' arms indelibly stamped with the stigmata of hate had made her especially fearful. Perhaps she was terrified that one day her children too would be seized as were her parents.

This is a country where Christians are a majority. It was in Christian Europe that her grandparents, uncles, aunts and all the other kin she would never know, had been put to death because they were not Christians. Would Christian Americans allow it to happen here? Would Jewish Americans submit?

Although the State of Israel now exists, a Jewish American feels strong ties of love and pride for his native country as do Jews of all the countries where they can live in peace. Language, locale, customs and culture endear themselves to the inhabitants whatever their race or religion.

That girl whose despair I witnessed was born in this country and wants it to be her own. Its language, customs, history and landscape are as familiar to her as to another girl her age, whose ancestors may have come here on the Mayflower.

Those occasional outbursts of antisemitism frighten her.

Must she as a Jew, always be on guard? Do we not all live in the freest, the most democratic of countries? And have we not been assured by the Founding Fathers that Church and State are forever separate; that no such destructive and ultimately totalitarian alliance can ever get a foothold here?

Will "they" ever let go? she asks mournfully. That speaker at the Holocaust meeting was trying to reassure her. But Jews with a long, bitter history of persecution are wary.

A 14th-century Jewish scholar wrote a letter to his co-religionists in Toledo, Spain warning them of imminent danger. Moses de Tordevillas reminded them that "Christian power can silence truth with a single blow." It was this power to silence truth that permitted the Church to persecute Jews for fifteen hundred years. Jews remain uneasy therefore until they are sure the Church can no longer inflict harm. Too much damage has been done and for too long for a daughter of death camp survivors to believe that a program of education and the good intentions of the best of Christians can be effective.

She would have been cheered, I think, by the words of a young woman who spoke out on the "Donahue" show. For his guests that day, Donahue had invited a group of bigots — I can't recall what their special target was. One of them during the show made a disparaging remark about Jews. With his uncanny ability to recognize the right speaker for the right moment, Donahue gave the floor to a hand-waver in the audience.

The young woman rose and in a strong emphatic voice said, "We are all Jews." A split second hush ensued. She continued. "I am a Roman Catholic and I know we are all children of God." She said a few more words in the same vein and sat down to warm applause.

Here I think of that speech which Pius XI made to a group of Belgian pilgrims. The invasion of Poland in 1939 was a year away. The Nuremberg Laws had been enacted in 1935. Jews were deprived of their citizenship. They were excluded from schools, jobs and all other activities. The Pope deplored Hitler's actions and the action of some German churches in allying themselves with him. He summed up the attitude of the Vatican in a sentence. "Spiritually (through Christ) we are all Semites."

I suppose Christian good will could go no farther. To say, "Spiritually we are all Jews" would have taken more courage than he had.

The present Pope has not recognized Israel, not only for fear of antagonizing the Arab nations. Catholic church doctrine argues that Judaism was only a way station on the path to the true faith, Christianity. With the advent of Christ, they assert, Judaism ceased to exist.

It was this anti-Judaic Christology that brought Auschwitz to pass.

Christology has been defined as the doctrine which declares that one aspect of God assumed a temporary form in the person of the Jewish preacher, Jesus. In this sonship aspect of God, this incarnation, Jesus obeyed the command of his Father to die a humanly agonizing death as a sacrifice to purify man of sin and grant him immortal life. If he had faith, that is.

As we may imagine, this doctrine has given theologians enough matter for centuries of argument and debate.

The Jewish religious authorities who encountered this thesis dismissed it. Most other Jews scattered over the Roman empire would have dismissed it too, had they heard of it. It would seem to be another form of paganism. Jewish religious history for a thousand years recorded the struggle against all forms of paganism which included the dying and resurrected god theme.

Israel learned early that God wanted obedience and trust, not human sacrifice when he stayed Abraham's knife. Abraham in obedience, had bound Isaac as he had been commanded though Isaac was his only son, the promise of future generations. A ram caught in the thicket nearby was the substitute.

Christology was not then—in the first century—and is not now a religion for Jews. Christians who do not question and who have been brought up to believe, find the concept right for them.

Great numbers of simple or fearful people still cling to the security of tradition and accept the dicta of those they consider their superiors in religious matters. But the better-educated and the independent thinkers are moving in another direction. Some churches seem to be following the lead of those younger more daring members who are turning more and more to the social gospel of Judaism — something they will find in their own "Old Testament." Except in very conservative and Fundamentalist Evangelical churches, the concern for personal salvation is taking second place to concern with the worldly needs of the oppressed, here and now.

Although changes are bound to come within the churches themselves, the most conservative still keep a tight hold on the Christology doctrine. Unfortunately this dogma carries within it, the anti-Judaism which is a necessary part of it. It is a serious dilemma for them. Without this creed, the churches might find themselves out of business.

If Jews were obliging enough to convert wholesale, the Church's problem would be solved.

Individual Christians are rarely interested in converting others unless theirs is a missionizing Church like the Mormon Church or Jehovah's Witnesses. There are some of course like that self-styled "Jesus freak" who got hold of me one day. She is an acquaintance, a friendly likable woman.

"We have so much in common," she began. "Jesus was a Jew, you know."

"I know," I say. "I've read the gospels. Everything he says is familiar to me from Judaism."

Irene is taken aback. She rallies however and prepares to go on. But I deliberately interrupt her. "There is one question I have."

"What is that?" Her attitude suggests there is no problem she can not overcome.

"Jesus Christ is your God," I say.

"God's only begotten son," she intones solemnly.

"And Christians believe he is God incarnate."

Irene nods agreement.

"We Jews," I tell her, "believe in only one God, God the Father, yours and mine. The question is, whatever can we do with an incarnation?"

Irene looks at me warily. "What do you mean?"

"We Jews," I say firmly, "do not believe that the one God of the universe can ever be cloned."

Irene is a good person. I like her but I have baffled her. She will not try again to convert me. And that is as it should be.

When I discovered that missionary groups to Jews were still functioning even after the Holocaust, I was shocked at the arrogance and the insensitivity of the churches that support such missions.

Paul and the early Christians had described the Jews as blind and stubborn for keeping to their beliefs and refusing to believe in a resurrected preacher who had died for man's sins. (Jews, it should be stated again, never thought that man was innately sinful. Only Paul thought of himself in this way.)

Surely Jews may apply the same adjectives "blind and stubborn" to those in the church who have not learned after two thousand years that conversion attempts are unprofitable and wasteful.

Certainly there are and have been voluntary Jewish converts. We may dismiss without comment those Jews who feel they may achieve by conversion some material goal otherwise denied them.

The really genuine converts from Judaism tend to be emotionally overwrought persons like the mystic, Raissa, wife of the theologian Jacques Maritain. A biographer notes in passing, that the couple lived a "pure," that is a non-sexual life.

Edith Stein, a nun and converted Jew, apparently chose death at Auschwitz. (It was at her memorial that Pope John Paul II knelt when he visited there in 1979.)

Simone Weill, a Frenchwoman died in her thirties, having effectively starved herself to death. Her biography suggests that she felt deprived and jealous of the attention given her handsomer and mathematically gifted brother. Apparently she turned against the Jewishness in herself (she was unmistakably "Jewish looking"), and moved to Catholicism, the prevailing religion of France. Because she always seemed on the verge of converting completely but never quite did, she engaged the absorbed attention of some deeply concerned priests. Her writing was anti-Judaic.

There are other examples of emotionally troubled Jews who have converted. I think with special concern of that tall, gaunt youth standing on the street corner opposite Macy's in Manhattan handing out leaflets. I took one. "Jews for Jesus," it said.

I had sent for their material earlier and had noted the superior paper on which their messages were printed, the good layout, the careful advertising techniques, the color. A well-financed organization, clearly. "Why this," I asked the young man. What about your Judaism?"

"Jesus was the perfect Jew," he mumbled uncomfortably. He turned away when I wanted to talk further with him.

Even though groups like "Jews for Jesus" use low key persuasion tactics, I regard them as predators. The "converts" I observed on their television program "Jewish Voice" stress the point that they are Jews; but they are "Messianic Jews," that is, they acknowledge Y'shua (never Jesus) as the messiah. The Protestant Fundamentalists that sponsor this mission seem in some respects like the cults even though their techniques are subtle and their grasp light. Their literature brims over with "Yiddishkeit"; their speakers are all Jews. There is something essentially dishonest about the whole enterprise, something evasive and devious.

That skinny, hollow-eyed young man seemed to be a helpless prey.

A church which professes to be sensitive to the needs of young people should direct that young man to a "habura" where he might be helped to find his own identity. Taking advantage of troubled youth is not an act of charity and lovingkindness. Will their converts eventually be required to accept a crucifix, symbol of Christian slaughter of Jews?

I do not believe that the Jew who converts to Christianity can find his answer there. For one thing, he would have to step over too many Jewish corpses.

There was another young Jew I encountered recently on a business matter. He was even taller and skinnier than the first but he had good posture, clear eyes and electric energy.

Perhaps because of my many years as an interviewer, perhaps because he was himself outgoing, we fell into easy conversation. I learned that he had joined an orthodox congregation and had become totally observant. His father a well-to-do businessman living comfortably in suburbia had scoffed at his son. He had certainly never given him any training or encouragement! The mother was not opposed; her father had been pious.

In our talk, I learned that the young man and his wife had

longed for a child. That very morning, he had learned that she was pregnant.

"I washed my hands, grabbed my prayer shawl and ran to the synagogue to give thanks," he said happily.

He mentioned also that in dining with some friends (vegetarians) he experienced a sense of emptiness even though the table was full of delicacies. "I missed the blessings," he explained.

Though I am not an observant Jew, like three-fourths of us here and in Israel, I was moved by that young man's recital. He had been converted, if that is the term, into his own faith. It was not in the nature of a "return" since he had had no experience or training in Judaism. It pleased him to belong now. He was studying Bible and Talmud, both revelations to him.

Heinrich Heine, the greatest of lyric poets had himself baptized in the first half of the 19th century, hoping thereby to get a university or government post closed to Jews. Deeply attached to his native country, he took on also the antisemitism of Germany. Being a Jew it became self-hatred. Yet he had feelings of both love and hate for his Jewish origins. "I was baptized," he is reported as saying, "but I was never converted." Heine loathed himself for his dishonesty. He became an exile in Paris, not having gotten a job in spite of his baptism.

Nineteenth-century Germany, always antisemitic, was cruel to its many gifted Jews. These were torn between their patriotic love for their fatherland and the torment of self-hatred forced on them by Jew-hating Germany. Baptism seldom solved their problems. Karl Marx whose parents had him baptized as a child, despised all religion as an "opiate" for oppressed people. Disraeli in England, though he was a powerful prime minister, beloved of Queen Victoria, was never regarded as other than a Jew.

In more recent years, Einstein and Freud, both secular Jews, never felt any need to separate themselves from their origins. Geniuses both, they must have felt indifferent to the clamor beneath their feet.

Some older readers may remember the Reverend Dr. John Hayne Holmes, pastor of the undenominational Community Church in New York City for more than four decades. A notable advocate of social justice, he was one of the founders of the

N.A.A.C.P. About the efforts of churches to missionize the Jews, he wrote indignantly, "it is as if they were heathen."

We can smile now at the word "heathen" and trust the Church no longer thinks in such antiquated terms of primitive peoples. Missionaries once did think of "heathen" as being in desperate need of salvation which only the one true faith could give them else they would burn in hell. The Catholic church relented only fairly recently and excused from eternal damnation those who were ignorant of the means to salvation through no fault of their own. But the Jews! There is no excuse for them.

We always have to remember that the Church is an establishment. One might correctly say that it is organized business. It collects revenues and dispenses jobs. (It does not pay taxes however.)

It differs from other businesses in the nature of the product it' offers, namely religion. This is an almost unbeatable commodity. In Protestantism, it has given rise to many competing denominations. Thus far, the Catholic church has maintained its monopoly. (From the climate in this country, I wonder when an American Catholic church will start its own liberal denomination.)

Regarded objectively, missionizing may be seen as a strategy to increase business. But if it were solely increased membership the Church wanted, it would not bother with the Jews; the effort and cash investment in missionary work would not be cost effective.

No, Jews are needed for other, more compelling reasons. Converted Jews would testify to the truth of their belief. That nagging sense of unfulfillment which theologians experience would be alleviated. Non-clerical Christians and even many liberal clergymen seem untroubled by the "unbelief" of Jews. But die-hard theologians and clerics persist. They do not realize that even if all Jews were eliminated, questioning Christian minds would continue to scrutinize their own dogma and doctrine.

A French Jesuit scholar, Joseph Bonsirven in his book *Palestinian Judaism in the Time of Jesus Christ* translated in 1964, shows us the mind of a devout Catholic who was troubled by this "unbelief." He took time and effort to read Jewish sources in Hebrew as well as the usual classic works in French and German.

What impressed me was his amazement as he discovered that

> "Nothing is more exalted and beautiful than Jewish ethics.
> It is loyal to the ideas expressed in the Old Testament and
> superior to all the ethical doctrines of antiquity. . . . in
> theory and practice, Jewish morality presents new features
> which show its excellence."

In addition to listing the many Jewish virtues (too long to
quote here), Father Bonsirven was amazed that the ideas were
not elitist but were embodied in the conduct professed and practiced by an entire people. Clearly the insights he gained through
his readings were new to him. He had not been exposed to any of
these in his training apparently.

The author concludes his book with a reproach. "Do we not
have a right to blame Judaism for having rejected Christ and his
message?" He believes that the Old Testament was intended to
pave the way for Christianity and he is upset that the "physical"
heirs of ancient Judaism did not recognize the one who was the
authentic, expected blossoming of their religion. He tries hard to
understand this Jewish lack of interest; he took the trouble to
study Judaism to find out. He discovered that Jews excelled in all
the virtues. Why then could they not have accepted Jesus as
savior? He seems baffled. How could such a moral people who
practiced righteousness, especially chastity (in which he seemed
particularly interested) remain Jews! He sounds not affronted but
aggrieved. He is deeply discouraged.

Jews are just as deeply discouraged by well-intentioned
churchmen like him who have "a veil over their eyes," to quote
Paul's misinterpretation. He can not rid himself of his narrow distorted view of Judaism.

He does not understand how Jews prefer to remain Jews. Rigidly indoctrinated as he was, he is unable to believe that any
other religion but his can have validity. In this respect his vision
is narrow, much narrower than Judaism's which has always held
that there is more than one way to the one God.

Earlier, I mentioned Franz Rosenzweig (1886–1929) regarded
as an innovative philosopher. Rosenzweig had lived in a totally

Christianized environment and was planning to become a Christian like his close friends. On the point of converting, this young intellectual decided to spend three months as a Jew first.

On the Day of Atonement in 1913, he attended services at an orthodox synagogue. The experience told him beyond the power of any words that he had found the center of his life in Judaism. He had what amounted to a conversion experience in which he recognized that his religious destiny belonged to his own heritage of over three thousand years.

Would Father Bonsirven, whose religious destiny was Christianity, recognize that equally religious Jews find their destiny in Judaism? Could he comprehend that a Jew can experience a deeply felt truth which is different from his truth? I doubt it.

He will continue, I think (and others will continue), to try to win Jews to his truth, which he sees as the only one. And Jews will continue to ignore these efforts. They have no religious reason to become Christian. This is not because of the Church's ignoble role in dealing with Jews, though this can not be erased from memory. Jews will not convert because they already have access to the Father through Torah and Talmudic wisdom. The concept of an entity which comes between him and his God is an alien one to a pious Jew.

Christians have no such insurmountable hurdle. For them Jesus or Christ is God. (Nowhere did Jesus make this claim for himself; St. John did.) There are some churches which deny Jesus' divinity altogether.

The majority of Christians appear to have accepted Jesus or Christ as God or God's son. True when the Trinity is invoked in any of the sacraments, God the Father is mentioned first. But generally he is given a back seat.

Perhaps the Almighty has been unpleasantly associated with the God of Abraham, Isaac and Jacob. Since for two millennia, Jews have been given a "bad press" by the Church, this God of Israel may be a bit of an embarrassment for theologians.

When those radical theologians broke into newsprint with their "death of God" books in the mid-60's, I believe it was the God of Abraham, Isaac and Jacob they wanted to scuttle. They toyed with the idea of unhooking Jesus from his Jewish moorings and floating off with him to some gnostic-type Christianity. These writers seem to have faded away.

I have noted that Christians as individuals are uninterested in or indifferent to theologic palaver. They seem unworried about the exact identity of Jesus. To Catholics, he is generally Christ the Lord God whose mother Mary is "Mother of God." To Protestants, especially the Evangelicals, he appears to be Jesus, a name to conjure with, to pray to, to worship, to have faith in. Even if he never existed, they would believe. The name Jesus is potent enough.

In time, the decision about belief will be taken out of ecclesiastical hands, I think. It is already ignored in many instances. Our best-educated young people — Jews and Christians — are marrying one another. Some figures say fifty percent. If they feel the need, they can begin a new religion, a really Jewish-Christian one perhaps with a platform that would include all the great positives and omit all the niggling negatives of religious thought and culture, that separate man from man and man from something loftier than himself.

As for the saying in Matthew (28:19), "Go therefore and make all nations my disciples. Baptize men everywhere in the name of the Father, the Son and the Holy Spirit," no thoughtful scholar believes that Jesus uttered those words, so patently anachronistic. It was Matthew, the promoter, who was far more interested in advancing the church than in accuracy. A little pious fraud was acceptable in such a worthy cause.

Here Matthew called on the authority of Jesus to further his aim of increasing membership. Trusting missionaries carried the Bible, unaware that they were spreading the "Christian disease fatal to Jews."

Not everyone brought up on the Christian Bible became infected. If they also had a loving home environment, they would tend to absorb the Hebraic-Christian morality they saw practiced. They might regard the ancient Jews as an extinct species like the Edomites or the Moabites.

Except that subliminally, a memory might persist. If they met a Jew, their immediate reaction might be wary or unfavorable especially since Jews have been presented with mindless irrationality over the centuries.

I recall an acquaintance who had received his early religious education from hostile, probably frustrated nuns, many years ago. One day, seated directly opposite him by chance, I noted his look when the toll of Jewish dead in the Holocaust was mentioned. He had quickly lowered his eyelids but not before I had seen the unmistakable glint of satisfaction in them. This expression of "unholy" joy in his eyes was involuntary and I am sure he was ashamed of it. But he had not overcome the indoctrination he had received as a young, deprived and unloved child from equally deprived and unloving nuns.

As for the New Testament with its vilification of Jews and its contrived passion story, its power to harm is mitigated, fortunately for all. Few read it. Priests and ministers usually try to avoid the hate-filled parts; even evangelicals administer only small safe doses.

To those of us, especially the Bible scholars, who know that the gospels were a planned work of deliberate missionizing, written by biased and fallible humans, we would expect that the first task of decent and caring Christians would be to purge it of its power to kill.

That girl who cried in despair, "They'll never let go of us," had probably never looked at a Christian Bible in her life. But she had experienced the hatred of which she and all Jews were the target.

X

TWO THOUSAND YEARS OF MYTH

"Well, what do you think?"

"About Christianity?"

"Yes, of course."

"I would say, off the top of my head, that Christianity is a delusion, a two-thousand-year-old delusion."

"You mean a hoax?"

"Not a hoax exactly, although its history contains many of these. It has been more like a misunderstanding, a mistake."

"That needs some explaining."

"I'll try."

About that long-lasting delusion, let me recapitulate my own understanding of how Christianity came about. It didn't just happen of course. It took a long time and hard work just as Judaism took a long time and hard work.

Here in summary is how I see it. Jesus, an obscure Jewish revivalist, preaches about a better world that is to come. The Roman rulers of that little province prick up their ears. Another rebellion in the offing? They take no chances and put this preacher to death just as John the Baptizer was put to death a year or more earlier under the same circumstances.

157

Five or maybe ten years later, an unhappy, guilt-ridden Greek-Jew named Paul hears about a charismatic preacher who was thought by some of his followers to have been seen <u>alive</u> after he was crucified.

Paul reacts with fierce anger when he hears this fantastic rumor of a resurrection. He over-reacts. Then, not unexpectedly, he reverses himself. He is struck by a daring idea, born of his desperation. What if God really cared enough for Paul to have a martyred fellow-Jew serve as a human sacrifice for the sin-beset Paul. A resurrection would be a real proof. Remember that these are apocalyptic, visionary end-of-the-world times. Anything is possible (here we can observe in Paul that trace of megalomania which often, as compensation, accompanies neurotic self-abasement).

Living in a pagan environment where mystery cults abound and where the folk mythology of death and resurrection is a commonplace, Paul's idea already has a structural framework.

He tries it out on his fellow-Jews. They dismiss it out of hand. For one thing, they are not afflicted with Paul's sense of sin and fear of death. But far more important, his idea is not the way of Torah. It was not for such a pagan idea that Jews suffered for more than a thousand years as they developed their concept of man's responsible relationship to God. Paul's idea that God would order an agonizing human sacrifice to atone for his sins was not only abhorrent in itself but it was a long step backward. The Jewish religious thinkers to whom Paul appealed turned away from him and his Hellenist frailty.

It should be noted that although Paul's monotheism was showing cracks, he could never, as a Jew, deify Jesus. The deification was left to the evangelist and former pagan John and to others who followed. Eventually Jesus was elevated from messiah (christ) to Lord, Savior and finally after three centuries to equality with God. (A number of churches do not acknowledge this doctrine.)

Rebuffed by his co-religionists, Paul turns to the Gentiles for reassurance. These have long admired Judaism; many have become near converts. When Paul abolishes circumcision and diet requirements for them, they join fully. They can have their cult and more important, they can have Judaism too.

Out in the world, the Jewish rebels have lost their last fanatic and futile battle against Rome. Beaten in war, they turn to their religion, purifying it and purging it of its apocalyptic accretions. Jewish faith becomes revitalized although their proselytizing efforts decline. Gentile missionaries continue their work vigorously after Paul's death.

Some shrewd administrators (like Matthew) as well as other earnest believers in the new sect promote it in earnest. They gauge correctly its good "growth potential."

They appropriate the Hebrew Scriptures in the Greek translation. They re-interpret them to make them seem like a prophesy foretelling the birth, death and rule of Jesus as messiah. They use whatever in prophets, psalms, proverbs, rabbinic wisdom they need in order to compose their New Testament. They m of available Jewish writing, generally in Greek translat few have any knowledge of Hebrew. They use and re apocalyptic and pseudepigraphic material which feed needs. To some they attribute Christian authorship.

In their New Testament, they flatter the Romans in order to appease them; they vilify the Jews whose treasures they have stolen; they invent a crucifixion scenario which libels and damns Jews even more venomously than the words they have Matthew and John put into Jesus' mouth. (The first of the evangelists, Mark, originated the Christ-killer motif, a falsehood which helped to delude Christians and which in time brought the Jews to Auschwitz.)

They "christianize" the synagogue service. The Jewish rite of immersion for cleansing and purifying the body becomes the baptism sacrament designed to remove sin. The Jewish Kiddush ceremony of giving thanks over bread and wine is converted into the eucharist (Greek for thanksgiving). Here the bread and wine is ingested by believers as if it were the body and blood of the sacrificed god. The believer is thus partaking of the god's immortality.

Christianity is now on its way to becoming a religion on its own. Church writers set to work to provide a respectable rationale for this strange hybrid, a Graeco-Oriental cult affixed like an ornamental veneer to a Judaic base.

Besides the baptism and eucharist rites necessary to provide converts with a sanctifying structure, the church leaders by the second century's end had gathered together and then selected four gospels. With Paul's letters, Luke's dubious and often fanciful history of the earliest years of the Church and some other letters, they now have their own Bible. This helps mark them off as a separate religion with a book of their own.

I think it was the scholar Krister Stendhal who once described a Christian as "a special kind of Jew." Perhaps in the very beginning he was. But I believe the two religions are incompatible entities. Jews must in honesty completely deny Christology as a concept forever alien to them since it expresses a pagan mythology. Christians to whom Christology is neither pagan nor alien can not give up this concept without denying the "sin and salvation" theory of the Church. Not all Churches define themselves thus, however.

Christology, as we said elsewhere, is that doctrine which proposes that God or an aspect of God was incarnated briefly in the Jewish preacher Jesus so he could die on the cross as a sacrifice to atone for the sins of those who believe he is Christ Jesus.

Enlightened Christians have long ago agreed that the whole schema is mythologic, a folkloric invention. The historian Arnold Toynbee, in a 1956 history, agreed that the story was a folk myth but he felt it had value. It could help man express the inexpressible. The legend of Jesus' death and resurrection while it parallels exactly the familiar myths of Osiris, Adonis, Tammuz and many such others has a symbolic value, he believes, since it celebrates the refructifying rebirth of the earth. The sacrificial death thesis has Paul's added component of expiated sin.

Jews, having recognized the pagan aspects of Paul's idea, would have been content to ignore it as an aberration of those troubled times. Unfortunately for Judaism and for mankind — civilization was retarded for more than a thousand years — the new sect could not let go. It needed Hebrew Scripture to "prove" its legitimacy. The means it took to achieve this end are briefly described in previous chapters. There will never be sufficient words to describe them fully.

Because the Church had to pretend that Judaism ceased to exist after the first century, you will not find in Christian history reference of any significance about Jews until perhaps the time that Protestant Bible scholarship began two centuries ago.

Reference to Jews in the Middle Ages have to do not with real persons but to those theological monsters called "Jews" to whom the evangelists and the Church Fathers gave birth.

Real Jews, a devout, civilized and literate people were seen in the distorted mirror of bedeviled and ignorant believers as monstrous accursed deicides. Jews were not the only victims of this appalling delusion. The victimizers themselves became victims. Originally undefiled children were deluded by lies into staining their hands with innocent blood as they grew up.

Although Jews were pushed out of world consciousness as much as possible, unless they were pulled out for an exile or a massacre, theologians always seemed to be aware of their existence. How could they not? Judaism has been a never healing canker in the flesh of Church theology. Jesus the Jew has served as a constant reminder that Christian theology will always have unfinished business.

Theologians have longed to be rid of the Jewishness of Jesus. Many of them argue that Jesus was in violent disagreement with important tenets of his Judaism; that he had actually forsaken his religion. Their arguments have invariably been found to be feeble, easily refuted by more competent scholars. Reputable scholars insist that any study of the historical Jesus must inevitably lead back to Judaism and only Judaism.

Those thousands upon thousands of books lying on dim shelves in countless libraries written by theologians, rarely read except on occasion by other theologians or students of religion, tell us of endless and fruitless arguments. We find empty and wasteful discussions about adoptionism or trinitarianism; we find debates between Arians and Athanasians; arguments about Nestorianism and Monophysitism. The Quartodecimans spent almost two hundred years quarreling as to whether Jesus' crucifixion took place on Passover day or Passover eve. This Paschal controversy which upset so many minds then, now appears absurd since it is reasonably certain that Jesus was not crucified on either of those dates.

To spend almost two millennia trying to justifying a pagan

mythology, a mistaken messiah belief, and a mistaken eschatology stupefies the rational mind.

Small wonder that the historian Dr. Muller called theology a "dreary, futile word game." I have spared the everyday reader such words as: kerygma, hermeneutics, pleroma, pneumatic, soteriology, kenosis, kairos, metanoia, homoousios and its kin homoiousios. Eisegesis looked like a new one. Exegesis and eschatology are common and convenient. Even paraclete and parousia have crept into fairly ordinary parlance. Generally, theologians keep their professional jargon for one another.

I sometimes wonder if theologians hide behind their vocabulary and make it esoteric and exclusive. It may be a convenient shorthand for others in the field or it may help lend an aura to their obscure subject matter by using Greek words. They do deal with the metaphysical, the supernatural and the questionable; it is difficult to be plain-spoken and clear in such matters.

That fourth century church reformer, St. John Chrysostom (he was, incidentally, named the patron of preachers in 1901 by a papal admirer) is well known by scholars in the field of anti-Judaism. He is the author of eight poison-dripping homilies against Jews, their synagogues and most especially the Judaizers, that is, the Christians in Antioch who joined them in their services, feasts and fast.

Frantic that these Christians who found Jewish services so attractive, might forsake their new faith, he wrote those sermons now famous as assisting countless thousands of Jews into the crematoria.

I have before me a 1973 book by a German theologian, Jurgen Moltmann. It is entitled *The Crucified God.* Sixteen hundred years after Chrysostom coined this pagan epithet "deicide," we find a modern book with such a pagan title! Apparently this theologian has held on to his pre-Holocaust mentality because an "overwhelming ideology" (to use Dr. Rubenstein's words) has succeeded in brainwashing him.

The Christian writer, Charlotte Klein said about most modern German theologians that their ignorance of Judaism was total. What they did learn was so distorted that it was worse than no knowledge at all. Moltmann with his "slain god" theology can not, it seems, extricate himself from that early indoctrination although his book does show the glimmering of an effort.

Two thousand years of church-controlled theology have added little to the advancement of liberated thought; it seems rather to place stumbling blocks in the way of progress. Theologians are generally establishment people. They are uneasy about disturbing the status quo. They want to keep their institution intact. Their livelihood depends on it and they find repose preferable to truth.

Here I do not refer to the numerous young-minded, open-minded truth seekers who are not afraid to take risks. Unfortunately the title "theologian" often gets attached to them.

Conservative, safe theologians like to delude themselves as they talk profoundly and comfortably in their ivied towers or plush church offices about the deep symbolic meaning of a crucified god. Here I would re-introduce my friend Abe. He it was who experienced reality stripped of any symbolic doubletalk. He termed the deicide accusation simply and accurately as "that deicide bullshit." Abe, I told you, is an outspoken man.

The question arises. How is it that Christianity (especially that of poor Catholics) seems to be so full of rites and ceremonies, saints, plaster figures, shrines and ikons, novenas, masses, feasts for this or that saint, crucifixes, holy pictures and much more of which I am ignorant. Why do so many pagan symbols fill their homes. Yet the cult does not die as did the ancient cults. The answer is of course to be found in the undying ethics of Judaism in Hebrew Scripture, in the liturgy adopted from Hebrew psalms, in the prayers and readings borrowed from Scripture. The New Testament when it is not taken up with vilifying Jews, also contains much of Jewish ethics. It is the Judaism in Christianity which keeps it alive in spite of the ornamental trappings placed over it.

"Judaism," says historian Dr. Muller (a Christian) "gave Christianity one God, a sacred book and the ideas for a New Testament. It contributed a historical tradition which made all life purposeful and all history meaningful. . . ."

"Hebrew Scripture was not a book of secret initiatory

rites for priests and theologians. It was an open book. By means of this book, the Christians could show their proselytes that they were not upstarts but the inheritors of an ancient sacred tradition, older than Rome itself. They had God's word, eloquent and explicit for his grand plan, his commandments and his covenants. Above all, they had a book magnificent in its own right, the greatest single work that man has produced. In spite of its unmystical and unmetaphysical spirit, the Old Testament reaches exalted conceptions of the unity of God and of man before God. Because of this spirit, it remains a rich source of inspiration for all men. . . ."

Beginning Christianity was fully aware that Judaism was the basic source of its strength. It needed however that mythological facing or overlay to appeal to its pagan converts. The early missionaries, beginning with Paul, really believed in the myth. Later, the more cultivated converts who became theologians for the Church, worked to find a philosophical ground for the mythical, supernatural belief, to reconcile if possible the dichotomy between faith and reason.

The historian Paul Johnson whose work we have mentioned earlier said that "Judaism might have become the universal religion for which the world longed had it not been tied to its barbarous umbilical cord." Diaspora Jewry might have succeeded he thought but the Palestinian Jewry of Jesus was too narrow and exclusive.

It seemed to be a closed community, strongly attached to Israel the land of its origin, and fearful of pagan influence which they had fought unceasingly for more than a thousand years before Paul and his pagan idea came on the scene.

Diaspora Jewry had already relaxed some of its ceremonial observances; Jews like Philo were students of classic Greek culture; Jews attended the sports gymnasia though this was not common.

Had Judaism become that world religion, a question comes to mind at once. Would the Jews have become corrupted by power as did the Church? One would recall the Hasmoneans in that short seventy year period when Judea was again an independent state. They were deposed because they had indeed become corrupted by power. They had assumed not only the temporal but the priestly power (as did the Church). Perhaps new prophets might have arisen as in centuries past to castigate the mighty. As it was, however, the quarreling allowed the Romans under Pompey to enter the province and place it under Roman rule in 63 B.C.E.

Could the Jewish religion have accommodated itself to the influx of Goths, east and west, to the Saxons, Gauls, Teutons, Huns, and Celts? Jews were brave and fierce fighters as their history confirms but would they not have tried other means to incorporate the strangers than by the sword? Would they have tried to eliminate paganism by education or would they have adopted it as did Christianity. Quoting Will Durant in his book *Caesar and Christ* "Christianity did not destroy paganism; it adopted it."

Had Judaism been able to retain its purity and integrity, we should have been spared the spilling of oceans and rivers of blood in crusades, inquisitions, heresy hunting and persecutions of Jews, other Christians and Moslems.

Would schisms have arisen as between the Eastern and Western Churches as they scrabbled over power? Would Islam have had to arise in response?

As one writer said despairingly, "Since Christianity has been a failure, why don't we try the religion of Christ." He did not have Judaism in mind but that precisely is what Jesus' religion was, Judaism.

With Judaism, education would have been a primary goal. Since with Jews religion and education are closely interrelated, civilization would have come more quickly to the world. That magnificent library in Alexandria of 700,000 manuscripts could never have been destroyed as it was under Christendom.

I recall the words of a medieval writer who refused to have his Latin book translated into the vernacular. "Too much light," he said, "is harmful for weak eyes."

Wyclif and his followers could not get the Bible translated into the vernacular in England until the 14th and 15th centuries.

Luther daringly translated the Bible into German in the 16th century.

To this day, there are conservative clergymen who object to having religious services conducted in the vernacular. (There are also among very orthodox Jews those who believe that the use of Hebrew for everyday speech is almost akin to blasphemy!)

The Hebraic concepts of brotherhood and equality finally broke through the darkness to give rise to the French Revolution. The Hebraic source of these concepts was not recognized nor acknowledged until fairly recently.

The church dogma of original sin, which kept the ignorant masses in a condition of terror, was their strongest weapon to keep man in a condition of serfdom (although many social and economic factors operated too): the belief in the divine right of kings; the superhuman power of the church over life or death in eternal fire; all these were exploited by a totalitarian church. Judaism to whom the notion of original sin, hell and damnation is utterly alien, could not but have been a great improvement.

St. Augustine, that most influential and most inhumane of Church Fathers (he seems also to have originated the idea of infant damnation), had no interest in improving the lot of the wretched poor. Life on earth was but a way station to the city of God. Why bother with worldly matters? Learning was discouraged and a century after Augustine, the emperor Justinian closed all the academies. "All the lights went out except that of faith, and the seal was put on the Dark Ages."

Sin and salvation, Christianity's winning hand, kept the masses painfully occupied during that millennium before they could stumble out of the Augustinian gloom into the light of emancipation. Once the premise is accepted that he is a sinner, man becomes a helpless seeker after salvation. The Church held before his eyes, that carrot of salvation. First, however, he had to allow himself to be laden, like a donkey, with the burden of sin.

Judaism denies the existence of original sin. It has always recognized that imperfect man has inclinations towards evil but he also has an inclination toward good. He must make his choice. Torah has taught him that the way of virtue is the way of life. And virtue is not only concern for his own well-being, although that is important, but more important, it means concern for the community.

Here the words of Hillel, the great sage of the first century B.C.E., may be apt. "If I am not for myself," he said, "who will be? But if I am for myself alone, what am I and if not now, when?"

> "Beginning with Moses," says Dr. Muller, "the gospel of the Hebrew prophets has always been a social gospel, not a means to private salvation. They were not saints bent on saving their immortal souls; they did not dwell on the ecstasies of their personal relation with God ... they themselves represented the highest ideals of Judaism, prophets exhorting their fellow men to follow God through righteousness. For the divine purpose as they conceived it in history could be fulfilled only by a community. The individual was not an end in himself. Judaism was unique in the idea of a dedicated community, a whole people that had a covenant or social contract, not a special favor but an awful responsibility. . ."

Judaism would have found no place for monasticism as an establishment. Monastic-like groups did exist as the Essenes, but they followed their own path unhindered, as was customary in Judaism. Had Judaism become a world religion, would it have had to set up a central authority as did Christianity? The idea seems strange and unacceptable. When Maimonides set up a creed in the 12th century, it became part of Jewish philosophy, never dogma. Jews have always resisted creed, doctrine and dogma. Judaism is simple and unhampered.

As for celibacy, this has always seemed an unwholesome aspect of the Catholic Church. It does have the effect of setting the celibate apart, granting him or her some special holiness as if the absence of sexual activity refined and purified one. This attitude harks back as far as Paul, the sectarians and the Church Fathers. Unfortunately, the celibate may sometimes develop emotional problems which also affect those he (or she) influences to their detriment. I have in mind some hostile nuns of long ago and some spinster teachers.

The veneration of saints, such an important part of Catholic activity seems like a modified form of polytheism. I know that the saint venerators enjoy this practice greatly. No one knows better than the Church that the practice is close to superstition as when a man will not board a plane unless he has his St. Christopher medal along. I sometimes think that the Catholic Church lacks genuine respect for its humbler members. Long centuries of ecclesiastical elitism may have something to do with this. Catholic clergy have traditionally kept themselves apart, not only as celibates (celibacy did not really become enforced until after the seventeenth century) but by their distinctive garb, their special titles, and by the aura of holiness they acquire. (Things have changed greatly it must be admitted, as we see young priests playing baseball in T shirts. Or working among the poor in the third world, a change which is not always approved by Rome.)

That the Catholic Church continues to countenance the veneration of relics, pilgrimages to shrines, the medieval belief in purgatory, penance and merits, all these and much more make me wonder whether the Church still considers itself king and the believers his subjects.

Things have changed of course and the Church would not, I think, approve of such medieval absurdities as when five churches in France each claimed to have the authentic foreskin from Jesus' circumcision. But the Church does not disapprove of fees charged by the archbishop of the cathedral in Turin so that people may view the shroud of Turin, as it is called. The money collected over the years, it is reported, helped build the cathedral. It continues to make money.

An American newspaper reporter interviewed the archbishop some years ago. The cloth had excited interest. Some gullible souls actually believed that the imprint on the shroud was that of Jesus after the crucifixion. People were not aware that a number of these cloths had been circulating in the 14th century and making a good deal of money for the clever artisan who had conceived and constructed the design.

True, the cloth was of great age but the archbishop courteously refused to have a tiny piece examined by modern methods to determine its real age. With a benign shrug, he explained to the reporter that it was important for people to believe.

Judaism did not become a world religion except in that it has profoundly influenced civilization through its legacy, the Hebrew Scriptures. These together with the Greek legacy of scientific inquiry have produced what small measure of progress man has made. Christianity in the form of an imperial church did what it could in those thousand years before the "emancipation" to hold back the advance, whether it was by gagging its great men like Galileo and Copernicus, by ignoring the needs of its impoverished and ignorant masses, or by terrorizing them with fear of hellfire. In spite of the Church, great minds emerged, great creative artists arose who used church themes, just as in ancient Greece, sculptors and architects like Phidias and Praxiteles made statues of their gods.

I am certainly unable to say how much better Judaism would have worked as a world religion. I can surely say it could not have been worse than Christianity. The record is there.

Given the fundamental difference between the two reluctantly related religions, is reconciliation possible? "Genuine rapport," says author F. Gladstone Bratton in his *Crime of Christendom* "can not come about until the effect of two millennia of mythological brainwashing is discarded."

The Catholic scholar Dr. Reuther in her *Faith and Fratricide* explains how the anti-Judaic tradition (with its mythological brainwashing) came about. The Church had to make its Christology legitimate by declaring it was proved by Jewish Scriptures; that these Scriptures were divinely intended to foretell Christianity; that the Jews in rejecting Jesus as Savior, did not understand their own Scriptures (emphasis mine).

> "As long as the 'Jews' . . . continue to reject this interpretation, the validity of the Christian view is in question. The 'wrath upon the Jews' poured out by Christianity, represents this ever unsatisfied need of the Church to prove that it has the true context of the Jewish Scriptures by finally making the Jews admit this is the true interpretation. Until Jewish religious tradition itself accepts this as

the 'real meaning' of its own Scriptures, 'the Jews' must be kept in the status of 'the enemies of God.'"

Thus writes Dr. Reuther in her *Faith and Fratricide,* the basic thesis of which is that "Anti-Judaism is the left hand of Christology."

The Church Fathers were concerned to prove that Jews in denying Jesus were therefore to be identified with the spirits of darkness; they were demonic, evil, carnal and unspiritual in contrast to the God of light, love and spirituality, as represented in Jesus. This theological Jew Devil which the Church writers concocted, this metaphysical monster of their frustrated imaginations was seen by simple believers as the real flesh and blood Jew. With such church interpretation, Christians might feel they had the church's tacit consent to kill Jews without guilt or remorse.

Dr. Reuther suggests that when Christianity is prepared to accept the idea that Judaism, in spite of its non-acceptance of Jesus, has an identity as a bona fide religion in its own right, then only can genuine dialogue take place.

I have mentioned the rigidly indoctrinated among the German clergy. There are many others in every country who can not relinquish their medieval ideas, who remain profoundly ignorant of Judaism.

And what shall we think of Pope Paul VI who addressed a parish on April 4, 1965 in a suburb of Rome telling the flock that after Christ was offered them, the Jews fought, slandered and finally killed him. His homily was reprinted the next day in the Vatican's L'Osservatore.

As long ago as 1927, the notable clergyman of the Anglican Church Rev. Robert Travers Herford—he is best known for his scholarly refutation of the false accusations about Pharisees in the gospels—wrote an essay in which he noted among other remarks that

". . . Christianity has not anything to offer the Jews of which they stand in vital need. As for converting, the Jews had everything to gain from a worldly point of view; from a spiritual point of view, they had nothing to gain and as the centuries passed, the Church had less and less that would induce a Jew to prefer Christianity to his own religion. . . ."

Dr. Herford urged reconciliation, even sympathy, remarking that it would help if the hard things written and spoken of old could belong to the old time. "Let the dead past bury its dead," he concluded.

Fifteen years later, the smoke began rising from the ovens of Dachau, Treblinka and Auschwitz.

The telephone repair man in our village is also the minister of a tiny evangelical church which functions on weekends. When he came to do some work, he noticed a framed print on the wall, a reproduction of a Jack Levine lithograph. It is a head of Shammai that pre-first century sage who usually argued the conservative position on religious matters with the more liberal Hillel.

"I see that you are one of God's chosen," the telephone man said.

"Not really," I murmured.

"Aren't you Jewish?"

"I'm a Jew, yes, but not many Jews believe they are chosen, except the more orthodox ones."

The weekend minister was puzzled. "If you're a Jew," he said after a moment, "then you're one of God's chosen. It says so in the Bible." And that was that.

I remembered a comment by a Jewish writer in a 1970 essay in which he declared that the Jews' chosenness is his "inescapable destiny."

I disagree with him totally as do most of the Jews I know.

Let us take a 3400 year leap back in time to the beginnings of Judaism, many centuries after the patriarchs, after Abraham and his covenant with God, to be sealed by circumcision (Genesis 17: 1-14). We find ourselves now among the tribes at the foot of Mt. Sinai or Mt. Horeb, whichever it was, where Moses is addressing the unruly crowds he has led out of captivity (Exodus 20).

Moses, a great man, perhaps the greatest teacher of all time, tells the tribes that their God Yahweh, the one and only God has agreed to a covenant with them. He will be their God and they will be his special people. Certain conditions in the form of commandments and prohibitions will be placed on them. These they must obey.

This covenant, a form of social contract, requires strict obedience to the will of Yahweh who demands righteousness, justice and care for one another. Each of these requirements is spelled out carefully and simply for the undisciplined tribes.

Moses, wise teacher, knows that either you live as a society which cares each for the other or you perish. The covenant he offered them was a technique for survival. The community, not the individual, was paramount. (Centuries later, Paul sacrificed this social gospel to his intense hunger for personal salvation. He thus weakened the moral vigor of the new religion he had inadvertently founded.)

By bestowing on an unformed people, the special "divine" attribute of "chosenness," Moses gave them a sense of worth, a sense of mission and the strength to endure the trials which accrue to the bearers of a holy burden. During the more than a thousand years in which the Jewish religion was being formed and solidified, their priests and prophets thundered and roared and howled at each transgression. They first castigated then comforted the peoples with promises of victory. In obeying the commands of the one God of the Universe, they were called "holy"; they were designated as a "nation of priests" and they were assured that they were God's "treasured possession."

Glancing at the long history of the Jews, we observe that their rewards were chiefly spiritual. It is this lofty spirituality which characterizes much of the Hebrew Bible. As for reward, perhaps Jews have won this in the knowledge that they have given the world the greatest possible gift, the Hebrew Scriptures.

During that first millennium after Moses, and during the two millennia during which Jews suffered Church persecution the sense of their chosenness must have helped them survive. They always nourished the hope that the Master of the Universe would never break the sacred inviolable contract or covenant.

The Holocaust changed the thinking of many Jews. The Holocaust event also changed the thinking of many sensitive Christians as well. Churches began, many for the first time, to examine themselves.

That phrase of Socrates, "know thyself" means searching one-self for signs of hubris or pride. Very few churches until recently searched themselves for hubris. Their stance was more often that of triumphalism.

Now nearing the start of its third millennium, the Church does seem in some instances to be turning inward to the strength of its Judaic component. Too many still cling to that Hellenist overlay, its Christology. For many thoughtful Christians, however, Christology appears to be waning in significance.

Many of us, Jews and Christians, have never accepted the metaphysics of religion, that is, man's assertions about matters which are now and may always be beyond comprehension; who have never regarded either Judaism or Christianity as "revealed" religions; who have not regarded Paul's resurrection-salvation thesis as anything other than the construct of a troubled mind.

As for Jesus' part in the myth built around his name, I regret that this revivalist preacher was so brusquely handled. For Paul, he served as a peg on which to hang his theory; for the synoptic gospelists, he was the subject of missionary tracts required for church purposes; for John, he was the manikin which he clothed to represent the god of that evangelist's own gnostic predilections.

That shadowy creature Yeshu/Jesus would indeed have re-mained a "buried footnote" if Paul had not conjured him up as the Christ figure he needed for his special schema.

What followed was both historical history and make-believe or theological history. The make-believe world of theological apolo-getics and polemics was designed, as we have learned, to justify and explain the violation and rape of Hebrew Scriptures. Real or historical history describes how the imperial Church put its theo-logical theory into punishing practice.

Those archaic and meaningless arguments about the univer-sality of Christianity versus the particularism of Judaism, the freedom to be found in Christ versus the legalism in Judaism, Christian love versus austere Jewish justice—these as well as other disputes which exercised theologians' minds, have no conceivable relevance now. I doubt that they ever did. Not only do they seem empty of content but often suspect as to intention.

We have to keep reminding ourselves that churches are business establishments, run by administrators who have a commodity to sell to a multitude of innocents who need to believe.

Genuine religious feeling is another matter. All of us experience this without having to connect it to deity. Here I remember the deeply felt comment in Yiddish of my mother. Listening to Bach, probably for the first time in her work-worn life, she murmured "himmeldick." It is Yiddish for "heavenly."

An exaltation of feeling whether it is in one's own creation or in experiencing the creation of another's work, has a quality of holiness. Attached to organized religion, this feeling may well get lost in rite and rote. We have only to think of commercial religion as it is beamed from satellites all over the world.

Dr. A. J. Heschel, the late scholar-thinker said: "As a tree torn from its soil, as a river separated from its source, so the human soul wanes when it is detached from something greater than itself." A devout Jew, he was thinking of God as that ineffable source.

Others may find their religious needs expressed in other ways than through God. Man's quest for meaning, his awe at the wonder of life and of all nature, including the marvel that is man, takes other paths.

The word "God" once described by the critic Edmund Wilson as "archaic," has indeed lost some of the creative holiness it once had.

I have watched and been entertained by televangelism, as it is called. Most of these are sponsored by Fundamentalist and Evangelical groups. I do not watch very long because I find them, for me, empty of content.

The speakers are often attractive and earnest; the stage is plush and flower-laden; the organist plays well; the quartet or choir of singers compares favorably with rock and roll singers and everyone appears to be blissfully happy.

The preacher will choose a line or a short passage from the Book, make a few forgettable comments, and then passionately urge his hearers to surrender to Jesus. Jesus will take all their troubles upon himself, including the pressing mortgage payment and the deadly cancer. He never directly promises a check for the house or a pill for the cancer but he does promise that wonderful feeling that comes from believing in Jesus.

They are then reminded to send that check or monthly pledge which insures the continuation of this vital program. A toll-free number is clearly printed on the television screen and in some programs, a bank of volunteers, their faces beaming with love and goodwill are awaiting your telephoned pledge. Other programs are of a different caliber, some offering counseling and making a less strident plea for money. But they do not vary too much. Good money is to be made here and the Christian network expands daily.

One morning as I was preparing breakfast, I watched a segment of the newscast. The date, of no special significance, happened to be 12/14/84 and the TV channel was either ABC or NBC.

A bearded young man, the leader of a group who somehow looked faceless was chanting a prayer with them; they were performing an act of faith, he explained (an auto-da-fé), preparatory to burning a batch of rock and roll records which they thought had some satanic content. This Christian cult got the publicity it wanted.

I, however, saw a group of black-garbed Dominican monks chanting the prayer, the auto-da-fé which preceded the sentencing of a "heretic" to death by fire. During Inquisition days, we would be smelling the odor of burning flesh; today it would be the toxic smell of vinyl rock and roll records.

The Church grew. It took the human Jew, Jesus and elevated him to godhood. The Gentile world was needy; it was more than willing to believe and worship. When the Jews found the Jewish preacher an unacceptable messiah, savior, intermediary between themselves and the Almighty, the new sect created the system of anti-Judaic polemic as its weapon against the unbelief of the Jews who rejected their Christ concept, their Christology.

Over the centuries, the Church provided splendid churches and cathedrals, a hierarchy of ecclesiastics, saints, relics and all the other accoutrements of religious worship.

Faith is more easily elicited and reinforced when accompanied, as in Catholicism, by the seductions of incense, candles, flowers, color, costumes, procession, uplifting music and narcotizing rite.

It must be faith surely which allows a Christian to read the paragraph below with an unblinking eye.

> "The ultimate miracle, the resurrection of Jesus Christ from the dead is recorded history. . . . It is the supreme proof of the divinity of Christ and is basic to all Catholic thought. Without this substantiation of His claim to divinity, all the other teachings of Christ would be invalidated and His death on the cross meaningless."

From "Catholicism" (p. 100) edited by Dr. G. Brantl, reprinted December 1967 by Washington Square Press, New York, N.Y. This paperback account of the most important of Catholic teachings received the "nihil obstat" of the Church book censor and the imprimatur of the then Archbishop of New York, Cardinal Spellman indicating that the book was free of doctrinal or moral error.

The Christological doctrine of sin and salvation kept needy and fearful believers on their knees; the Judaic infrastructure kept the Church on its feet. The Hebrew Bible and the Judaic moral and ethical underpinning found its way into the New Testament presumably via the oral tradition of Yeshu/Jesus.

The anti-Judaic polemic and the fiction of the passion play created by the evangelists gave rise to the unholy Christian disease.

Humankind, however, produced a holiness of its own, the holiness of creativity in science, music, art, literature and loving.

Anti-Judaism will no longer provide nourishment for a mythic Christology. Enlightened Christians, both lay and clerical, scholars and historians are best qualified to cure the disease. Most Jews, many of whom have been wounded beyond healing, will cooperate but the greater task belongs to a Christianity which must purge and purify itself of a long sickness.

Afterword

The Gospels were written between the years 70 to 120 by earnest believers who missionized zealously in behalf of the new, weak Gentile Church. (The Gospels along with Paul's letters, Luke's "Acts of the Apostles" and some other brief writings make up the New Testament.)

In addition to providing a much needed, uniform handbook for members, converts and proselytes, the gospel writers had other important aims: Jesus had died about the year 30; the Jerusalem Temple had been destroyed in the year 70. It was time now to carry out those missionary aims: to distance the new sect from the rebellious Jews; to court the favor of Rome and most of all to disparage and denigrate the strong, legally established religion of the Jews while at the same time arrogating to itself the thousand year old treasures of the Hebrew Bible as well as more recent Jewish writings.

These are the facts. It is also a fact that the New Testament writings are posited on the theories of Paul in whose epistles, the theme of human sacrifice and resurrection suggested the plot for the crucifixion drama as well as for basic Christian theology.

Human sacrifice, long discarded by Judaism as a barbaric remnant of a primitive pagan past, had been seized upon by Paul, the Hellenist Jew, given a quasi-theologic coating and then adopted by this emotionally troubled man in his frantic search for personal salvation.

With human sacrifice came the typically pagan deification of the sacrificed one. This was done with Jesus.

The missioning evangelists had to have recourse to inventions, distortions and misstatements to achieve their aims. In the matter of the crucifixion story, the gospelists resorted to outright lies and false accusations. The crucifixion melodrama persists to this day as if it were actual history. Yet all anyone knows is that a certain Jesus was put to death by crucifixion. Exactly when, where and why this event took place is unknown and may never be known exactly. One can only surmise.

Although the Jesus-Christology myth is losing its hold among better-educated and thoughtful Christians, including some in the clergy, it is still a matter of belief among millions of others who are being daily indoctrinated.

On March 31, 1985, the CBS television program "Sixty Minutes," presented a segment on a "trade show" by and for Christian groups who were engaged in buying and selling television time for their product, namely the Evangelical, Fundamentalist or Pentecostal message. There were other, similar groups whose church affiliation I did not learn.

Such groups are now big business with hundreds of millions of dollars, all tax free, being gathered in from television viewers by aggressively competing preachers.

One youngish man was being questioned by the CBS reporter Morley Safer. In reply, the interviewee said that yes, all those who did not accept Christ as their savior were destined for hell. These included Moslems and Jews.

"Jews?", queried the reporter.

"Yes," the youngish man answered. Then presumably as an after-thought, he added "They are of their father the devil."

We note that in chapter 8, verse 44 of the gospel of John, Jesus is made to address his fellow Jews with the words: "Ye are of your father the devil". John wrote his gospel about 1900 years ago; his words have not been forgotten.

The crucifixion story is even more deadly. It contains within itself the seeds of evil. These have been germinating and bearing fruit over the centuries. But they burst into full flower in the Holocaust.

As long as the Church presents a theology of a deified god of light in contrast to the Jew as the embodiment of evil and darkness, so long will the possibility exist that a Jewish child may once more be tossed alive and screaming into a blazing bonfire and a Jewish infant hurled to its death against an electrified fence.

The educational campaign waged by genuinely religious and honorable Christians (like Dr. Eugene Fisher of the Bishops' Secretariat for Catholic-Jewish Relations) and many others both Catholic and Protestant, is helpful. But can it ever be enough?

We need to draw back a moment and reflect. There dwells in all humankind that *yetzer ha ra*, the evil inclination of which the rabbis spoke. We read in Torah (Gen. 4:7) "Sin is the demon at the door whose urge is toward you, yet you can be his master."

The task of religious teaching is helping humankind overcome its *yetzer ha ra*, its sin of hating.

But two thousand years of inculcated Jew hatred, a sanctioned, even a sacred hatred, can this be overcome by education?

When the Jewish religious authorities, almost two thousand years ago rejected the Christian myth, they were heeding the wisdom of the great Hebrew prophets who thundered against the paganism inherent in human sacrifice and deification. They understood its regressive nature. Jesus would have called it sacrilege. Gentiles however could accept a familiar pagan theme. They celebrate this theme every Easter.

I do not despair. As a Jew, I am the eternal optimist. I believe that the Christology concept will gradually fade away and disappear. The signs are here.

The Christian Bible contains morality, ethics and wisdom in its parables, beatitudes and other teachings. No matter that they are derived from Hebraic and rabbinic sources; these too are now part of Christianity. Enough true religion inheres in that heritage so Christians can safely advance beyond the myth of Christology.

BRIEF BIBLIOGRAPHY

Agus, Jacob B. *Dialogue and Tradition*
   (London: Abelard-Schuman, 1971)
Baron, Salo W. *Social and Religious History of the Jews*
   (New York: Columbia Univ. Press, 1958–60)
Bevan, Elwyn and Sir George Adam Smith. *The Legacy of Israel*
   (Oxford: Clarendon Press, 1927)
Bokser, Ben Zion. *Judaism and the Christian Predicament*
   (New York: Knopf, 1967)
Bratton, Fred G. *The Crime of Christendom*
   (New York: Beacon Press, 1969)
Cohen, Arthur A. *The Myth of the Judeo-Christian Tradition*
   (New York: Harper & Row, 1970)
Davies, Alan T. *Antisemitism and the Christian Mind*
   (New York: Herder & Herder, 1969)
————. *Antisemitism and the Foundations of Christianity*
   (New York: Pauline Press, 1979)
Eckardt, A. Roy. *Your People, My People*
   (New York: Quadrangle, 1974)
————. *Elder and the Younger Brothers*
   (New York: Schocken Books, 1973)
———— and Alice L. Eckardt. *Long Night's Journey Into Day*
   (Detroit: Wayne Univ. Press, 1977)
Enslin, Morton S. *Christian Beginnings*
   (New York: Harper & Row, 1938)
Fisher, Eugene. *Faith and Prejudice*
   (New York: Paulist Press, 1977)
Gavin, F. *The Jewish Antecedents of the Christian Sacraments*
   (New York: KTAV, 1928)
Gordis, Robert. *Judaism in a Christian World*
   (New York: McGraw-Hill, 1966)
————. *The Root and the Branch: Judaism and the Free Society*
   (Chicago: University of Chicago Press, 1962)
Grant, Frederick. *Ancient Judaism and the New Testament*
   (New York: MacMillan, 1959)
Grant, Michael. *The Jews in the Roman World*
   (New York: Scribner's, 1973)
Grant, Robert M. *Early Christianity and Society*
   (San Francisco: Harper & Row, 1977)
Grosser, Paul E. and Edwin G. Halperin. *Antisemitism*
   (Secaucus, N.J.: Citadel Press, 1979)
Hay, Malcolm. *Europe and the Jews* (former title — *Foot of Pride*)
   (Boston: Beacon Press, 1961)
Herford, Robert Travers. *The Pharisees*
   (New York: MacMillan, 1928)
Isaac, Julius. *The Teaching of Contempt*
   (New York: McGraw-Hill, 1965)
Johnson, Paul. *A History of Christianity*
   (New York: Atheneum, 1979)
Kaufmann, Walter. *The Faith of a Heretic*
   (Garden City: Anchor Books, 1963)

————. *Critique of Religion and Philosophy*
(Garden City: Anchor Books, 1961)
Littell, Franklin. *The Crucifixion of the Jews*
(New York: Harper & Row, 1975)
Loewenstein, Rudolph M. *Christians and Jews, A Psychoanalytic Study*
(New York: International Press, 1958)
Memmi, Albert. *Portrait of a Jew*
(London: Eyre & Spottiswoode, 1963)
————. *The Liberation of the Jew*
(New York: Orion Press, 1966)
Moehlman, Conrad H. *The Christian-Jewish Tragedy*
(Rochester: Leo Hart, 1933)
Moore, George Foot. *Judaism in the First Centuries of the Christian Era*
(Cambridge: Harvard Univ. Press, 1927–30)
Muller, Herbert J. *Uses of the Past*
(New York: Oxford Univ. Press, 1957)
Oesterley, Wm. O. E. *Jewish Background of Christian Liturgy*
(Oxford: Clarendon Press, 1925)
Olson, Bernhard E. *Faith or Prejudice*
(New Haven: Yale Univ. Press, 1963)
Parkes, James William. *The Conflict of the Church and the Synagogue*
(New York: Meridian Books, 1961)
————. *Prelude to Dialogue: Jewish Christian Relationships*
(New York: Schocken Books, 1969)
Rubenstein, Richard L. *After Auschwitz*
(Indianapolis: Bobbs-Merrill, 1966)
————. *The Cunning of History*
(New York: Harper & Row, 1975)
Ruether, Rosemary. *Faith and Fratricide*
(New York: Seabury Press, 1974)
Sandmel, Samuel. *The First Christian Century in Judaism and Christianity*
(New York: Oxford Univ. Press, 1969)
————. *The Genius of Paul*
(New York: Farrar, Straus & Giroux, 1958)
————. *A Jewish Understanding of the New Testament*
(New York: Hebrew Union College Press, 1943)
Shoeps, Hans Joachim. *The Jewish Christian Argument*
(New York: Holt, Rinehart & Winston, 1963)
Selznick, Gertrude S. and Stephen Steinberg. *The Tenacity of Prejudice*
(New York: Harper & Row, 1969)
Strack, Hermann L. *Introduction to the Talmud and Midrash*
(New York: Atheneum, 1974)
Tcherikover, Victor. *Hellenistic Civilization and the Jews*
(Philadelphia: Jewish Publication Society, 1959)
Trachtenberg, Joshua. *The Devil and the Jews*
(New York: Harper & Row, 1966)
Woods, James E. (ed.) *Jewish-Christian Relations in Today's World*
(Waco, Texas: Baylor Univ. Press, 1971)

CORRECTIONS

Page 11—correct spelling is <u>Ruether</u>
Page 12—<u>Aramaic</u> is a relative, not a
        dialect of Hebrew
Page 31—8th line from the bottom
        <u>the the</u> should be <u>that the</u>
Page 67—4th line from bottom
        <u>every</u> should be <u>ever</u>
Page 110—correct spelling is
        <u>idolaters</u>
Page 122—quotation from Nietzsche
        correct word is <u>arrogated</u>,
        not <u>abrogated</u>
Page 126—correct spelling is <u>idolaters</u>
Page 126—4th paragraph down
        correct word is <u>after</u>,
        not <u>before</u> the "proofs"